SPSS® LISREL® 7 and PRELIS™ User's Guide and Reference

LAMBDA X

	KSI 1	KSI 2
VAR 1	0.4116	0.0000
VAR 2	0.3336	0.0000
VAR 3	0.0000	0.4637
VAR 4	0.0000	0.3630
VAR 5	0.0000	0.7761
VAR 6	0.7911	0.0000
VAR 7	0.3027	0.0000
VAR 8	0.0000	0.7052

SPSS

SPSS Inc.

SPSS Inc.
444 N. Michigan Avenue
Chicago, Illinois 60611
Tel: (312) 329-2400
Fax: (312) 329-3668

For more information about SPSS® LISREL® 7 and PRELIS™ User's Guide and Reference software products, please write or call

Marketing Department
SPSS Inc.
444 North Michigan Avenue
Chicago, IL 60611
Tel: (312) 329-2400
Fax: (312) 329-3668

3 4 5 6 7 8 9 0   95 94 93

ISBN 0-918469-70-8

Library of Congress Catalog Card Number: 89-069859

Preface

SPSS LISREL is an optional extension of the SPSS system, available with Release 4 of SPSS on selected computer systems. It consists of two procedures, PRELIS and LISREL, which contain powerful techniques for analyzing linear structural relationships.

PRELIS

PRELIS, a preprocessor for LISREL, greatly improves and accelerates analysis of binary, categorical, ordinal, censored, continuous and/or incomplete data. PRELIS enables LISREL users to achieve more accurate and powerful analyses than have been possible before. But PRELIS can also provide a first descriptive look at raw data even when no LISREL analysis is intended, or when analysis will be done with other programs.

Experience in consultation with users of LISREL has shown that they are not always sufficiently familiar with characteristics and problems of their raw data when they set out to estimate and test a LISREL model. Problems in the raw data can often account for peculiarities that occur when estimating and testing LISREL models.

PRELIS does a fair amount of data screening, and has been prepared in the spirit of Tukey's (1977) principle: "It is important to understand what you *can do* before you learn to measure how *well* you have *done* it." It also increases the analyst's awareness of scale types and distribution of variables (both individually and jointly) and the distribution of missing values over variables and cases.

PRELIS can read raw data on continuous, censored, and ordinal variables. It can compute many different measures of association between pairs of such variables. In some cases, PRELIS can provide an estimate of the asymptotic (large sample) covariance matrix of such measures. These can be used in LISREL 7 to perform a more accurate and powerful analysis than has been available with previous versions of LISREL.

LISREL 7

The most useful and accessible techniques of statistical analysis are those that estimate and test linear relationships among variables. Typically, the investigator wants to determine the coefficients of simultaneous linear equations relating the dependent or response variables to the independent or explanatory variables. It is well known that, when the independent variables are measured without error, multivariate least-squares or maximum likelihood regression techniques serve this purpose very well. But when the independent variables are measured with error, the so-called "errors-in-variables" problem arises and the estimates of the regression coefficients are biased.

Professor Karl Jöreskog of the Department of Statistics, Uppsala University, Sweden, has provided the most comprehensive solution to the errors-in-variables problem with his LISREL model. It combines multivariate measurement models for the dependent and independent latent variables with recursive or non-recursive models for linear relationships between latent variables.

Version 7 of the widely used LISREL program, extensively revised and updated by Karl Jöreskog and Dag Sörbom, puts new facilities for data analysis in the hands of SPSS users. This SPSS LISREL 7 and PRELIS manual is accompanied by a completely new 342-page textbook, entitled *LISREL 7: A Guide to the Program and Applications.* This text, along with the more than 70 sample problems that are supplied with the program, provide step-by-step instruction in LISREL analysis and its interpretation in realistic settings.

New Features

Several enhancements have been made to the LISREL procedure since it was first offered as an SPSS option (USERPROC LISREL). Version 7 of LISREL has the following new features:

- Two new estimation methods, weighted least squares (WLS) and diagonally weighted least squares (DWLS), have been added.
- Models with mean parameters (intercept terms) and mean values of latent variables may now be specified directly.
- Standard errors are calculated for total and indirect effect-size estimates.
- Standard errors, *t*-values, standardized residuals and chi-square goodness-of-fit values may now be obtained for the unweighted least squares (ULS) method.
- A new Ridge Option for handling covariance and correlation matrices that are not positive-definite. The Ridge Option is particularly useful for econometric models containing identities and for regression models with high multicollinearity among the regressors.
- New and improved algorithms for instrumental variables (IV) and two-stage least squares (TSLS) estimation.
- Calculation of standardized residuals based on more general assumptions.
- Modification indices for all iterative estimation methods.
- Stem-and-leaf plots for residual analysis.
- Parameter plots.
- An admissibility check of the model with options to stop before iterations begin.
- New informative error messages and tighter syntax checking.

Acknowledgment

Preparation of this manual, including extensive revision of the original documentation to accord with the syntax and operations of the software within SPSS, was carried out for SPSS by Leo Stam, under contract with Scientific Software, Inc.

Additional Documentation

SPSS is supported by other manuals that supplement this document in the area of statistics and applications. First, the manuals for the Base System. Documentation for SPSS Release 4 consists of three parts:

- User's Guides.
  - *SPSS Base System User's Guide* shows how to use SPSS commands to manage and analyze data. It explains many of the statistical concepts involved and includes brief operational instructions for each command.
  - *SPSS Advanced Statistics User's Guide* extends the SPSS Base System User's Guide to cover advanced statistical procedures.
- *SPSS Reference Guide* documents and gives examples of all of the commands, subcommands, and keywords in the base system and Advanced Statistics option.
- An operations guide tells how to run SPSS on one of the operating systems for which the software is available, and explains any differences between that version of SPSS and the system as documented in the user and reference guides. The following operations guides are scheduled for availability in 1989 or early 1990: SPSS for OS/2, SPSS for the Macintosh, SPSS for UNIX, SPSS for IBM/CMS, and SPSS for VAX/VMS.

The following manuals discuss options in addition to LISREL and PRELIS available for most versions of SPSS. Not all options are available for all operating systems.

- *SPSS Trends*™ documents SPSS's complete time series analysis and forecasting tool. The Trends option includes curve fitting, smoothing, special regression, seasonal adjustment, and Box-Jenkins/ARIMA modeling procedures. The manual contains sample applications and a complete reference to the commands in the Trends option.
- *SPSS Tables*™ documents the SPSS TABLES procedure, which presents data in presentation quality tables. TABLES can tabulate multiple variables at once and provides great flexibility for displaying totals, percentages, and other statistics. The SPSS Tables manual includes a user's guide and a complete reference to TABLES subcommands.
- *SPSS Categories* documents the three conjoint and four correspondence analysis procedures in this new option. The manual includes illustrative applications and a complete reference to the commands.

Contacting SPSS Inc.

The SPSS system is constantly undergoing enhancements. For additional information about your system, including any updates since the printing of the most current version of the manual, use the INFO command documented in the reference guide. If you would like to be on our mailing list, write to us at one of the addresses on the next page. We will send you a copy of our newsletter and let you know about SPSS Inc. activities in your area.

SPSS Inc.
444 North Michigan Ave.
Chicago, IL 60611
Tel: (312) 329-2400
Fax: (312) 329-3668

SPSS Federal Systems
12030 Sunrise Valley Dr.
Suite 300
Reston, VA 22091
Tel: (703) 391-6020
Fax: (703) 391-6002

SPSS Latin America
444 North Michigan Ave.
Chicago, IL 60611
Tel: (312) 329-3556
Fax: (312) 329-3668

SPSS Benelux BV
P.O. Box 115
4200 AC Gorinchem
The Netherlands
Tel: +31.1830.36711
Fax: +31.1830.35839

SPSS UK Ltd.
SPSS House
5 London Street
Chertsey
Surrey KT16 8AP
United Kingdom
Tel: +44.932.566262
Fax: +44.932.567020

SPSS UK Ltd., New Delhi
c/o Ashok Business Centre
Ashok Hotel
50B Chanakyapuri
New Delhi 110 021
India
Tel: +91.11.600121 x1029
Fax: +91.11.6873216

SPSS GmbH Software
Steinsdorfstrasse 19
D-8000 Munich 22
Germany
Tel:+ 49.89.2283008
Fax: +49.89.2285413

SPSS Scandinavia AB
Sjöängsvägen 7
S-191 72 Sollentuna
Sweden
Tel: +46.8.7549450
Fax: +46.8.7548816

SPSS Asia Pacific Pte. Ltd.
10 Anson Road, #34-07
International Plaza
Singapore 0207
Singapore
Tel: +65.221.2577
Fax: +65.221.9920

SPSS Japan Inc.
Gyoen Sky Bldg.
2-1-11, Shinjuku
Shinjuku-ku
Tokyo 160
Japan
Tel: +81.3.33505261
Fax: +81.3.33505245

SPSS Australasia Pty. Ltd.
121 Walker Street
North Sydney, NSW 2060
Australia
Tel: +61.2.954.5660
Fax: +61.2.954.5616

Contents

Introduction

Contents

About This Manual

This manual is divided into several parts that provide information for both new and experienced users. One important part seems missing from the contents outlined below, *i.e.*, a LISREL User's Guide. Since the LISREL approach has been extensively documented in a new textbook, *LISREL 7: A Guide to the Program and Applications,* written by Jöreskog and Sörbom (1989, 2nd edition) and distributed by SPSS Inc., this manual concentrates on the LISREL subcommands.

The filenames shown in the examples generally follow IBM/CMS conventions. The user should replace them with filenames that agree with the specifications of his operating system.

Introduction. Besides the section you are reading now, Part A contains a description of how PRELIS and LISREL work within an SPSS job. First, it discusses briefly the implementation of the PRELIS and LISREL stand-alone versions in the SPSS system. Secondly, it addresses such questions as, "If I have a file containing a number of related variables, how do I set up a job to analyze them with LISREL?" "Is PRELIS always necessary?" With sample jobs the various ways that data can be input are illustrated. Next, the SPLIT FILE feature of SPSS is discussed in relation to PRELIS and LISREL. For the user who knows native LISREL syntax, a final section draws attention to some finer consequences of the SPSS implementation.

PRELIS User's Guide. The PRELIS User's Guide, Part B, discusses the different variables that PRELIS can handle, the various types of moment matrices it can compute, as well as the special weight matrices that are needed for certain fit functions in LISREL.

PRELIS Subcommand Reference. The main ingredient of the PRELIS Subcommand Reference, Part C, consists of separate sections that describe each PRELIS subcommand in detail, using brief examples if necessary. It is followed by a PRELIS command syntax overview.

LISREL 7 Subcommand Reference. Part D likewise describes each LISREL subcommand in detail and ends with a LISREL command syntax overview.

Examples. The examples in Part E are mainly PRELIS examples, because the LISREL textbook mentioned above contains an abundance of LISREL examples (Appendix 2 has a selection of those examples, adapted to make them run within SPSS). However, to guide the reader, one annotated LISREL example has been included. The second section of Part A also contains several examples, illustrating specifically how to run PRELIS and LISREL in tandem.

PRELIS and LISREL within SPSS

LISREL was first introduced to the SPSS user as USERPROC LISREL, containing the LISREL 6 version. The new PRELIS and LISREL 7 procedures described in this manual may appear to the SPSS user as an upgrade to full-fledged SPSS procedures. However, this is not entirely the case. Karl Jöreskog and Dag Sörbom created both programs, and they will continue to maintain and to develop them further as stand-alone versions. SPSS has added an interface—or shell—for both programs, such that the SPSS user has access to PRELIS and LISREL from within the SPSS system. Among other things, the interface will translate the user input, *i.e.*, the subcommands with their specifications, into the appropriate native PRELIS or LISREL command lines, and from there the original software product will take over.

In developing such an interface, one of the decisions to be made is whether the procedure should resemble other SPSS procedures, or whether the syntax of the original program should be left untouched as much as possible. Because the native LISREL syntax is already widespread in the literature, it was decided to follow the last route for this procedure. In fact, only one subcommand was added, to allow for SPSS (matrix) system input. The PRELIS interface follows the first route and implements typical SPSS subcommands, which means that the user who is familiar with native PRELIS commands has little advantage over the new user of the SPSS version. Fortunately, there are not many subcommands in the SPSS PRELIS procedure. The user who is familiar with the native LISREL syntax, on the other hand, will feel "almost at home." Command Files that were written for the stand-alone version could be used in the SPSS system with very minor changes. A look at the examples in this manual (see, for instance, Part E) will make that clear. Often, some extra changes are needed to use the SPSS system in a more advantageous way, which is why we focus below on the various ways that data can be input and on the SPSS SPLIT FILE feature.

In this manual the term "raw data" is used in contrast with "summary data" like correlations, moments or covariances. "External file" refers to a data file that is *not* an SPSS system file. Filenames in the examples are generally given in accord with IBM/CMS specifications; the user should replace them with names that agree with the conventions of his operating system.

Data Input

Figure A–1 gives an overview of the different ways data can be prepared for a LISREL analysis. Starting from a raw data file, the recommended path towards a LISREL analysis is: create an SPSS (active) system file, then use the PRELIS procedure to produce a matrix system file, which will then be the data source for LISREL. The alternative way, instructing LISREL to read the raw data directly (using the LISREL RA subcommand), is possible for the analysis of product moment correlation, covariance or moment matrices. If an active file with the raw data has been created, the SPSS LISREL interface will set the RA and LA subcommands in LISREL.

The user who follows this alternative path has limited the possibilities. If there are missing values in the data, then the only option left is listwise deletion. Both user missing values and system missing values will be treated as missing. For the possibility of pairwise deletion the PRELIS procedure should be used. PRELIS is also needed when the user contemplates either generally weighted least-squares analysis or diagonally weighted least-squares analysis. These LISREL methods (WLS and DWLS keywords on the OU subcommand) require a sample asymptotic variance or covariance matrix. The PRELIS procedure is able to estimate these weight matrices, and writes them in a format that LISREL will read. Finally, the recommended path through PRELIS also becomes a required path when the data contain ordinal variables and product moment correlations are not justified. PRELIS offers the possibility of polychoric and polyserial correlations, as well as correlations based on optimal scores (sometimes called canonical correlations), or normal scores (see p. B–4). It also handles censored variables.

Figure A–1. Pathways from data to LISREL.

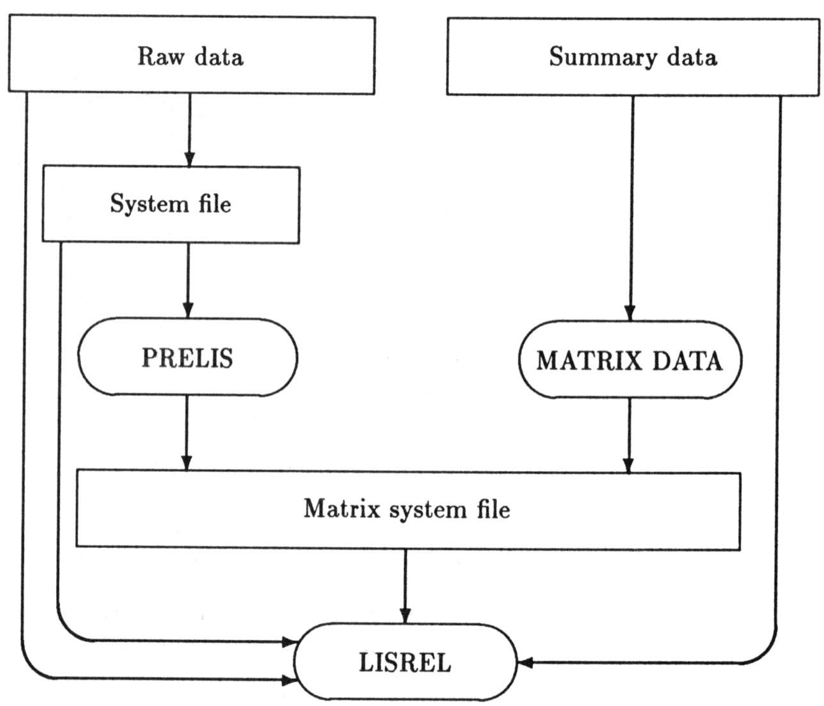

Obviously, a path not given in Figure A–1 runs from the SPSS system file towards LISREL via some other procedure than PRELIS. With the procedure CORRELATIONS a matrix system file of Pearson product moment correlations is easily produced, but at no particular advantage. It is also possible, of course, to use the summary data matrix produced by PRELIS as input for other SPSS procedures.

The following example follows the recommended path. The matrix system file created, although active, is mentioned explicitly. Since this is the default, in both PRELIS and LISREL the MATRIX subcommand could have been omitted.

```
DATA LIST FILE='RAW DATA' FREE /1 VAR1 VAR2 VAR3 VAR4
PRELIS
   /VARIABLES=VAR1 TO VAR4
   /MATRIX=OUT (*)
   /TYPE=COVARIANCE
LISREL
   /MATRIX=IN  (*)
   /DA NI=4
   /MO NX=4 NK=1 LX=FR PH=ST
   /OU
FINISH
```

In the next example an SPSS system file is created from a raw data file in fixed format, and PRELIS is used to create a matrix system file containing the correlations. This matrix system file will be saved for further use, because the MATRIX subcommand specifies a named output file.

```
DATA LIST FILE='PRL_RAW INPUT' FIXED RECORDS=1
   / HUMRGHTS 1 EQUALCON 2 RACEPROB 3 EQUALVAL 4 EUTHANAS 5
     CRIMEPUN 6 CONSCOBJ 7 GUILT 8
MISSING VALUES HUMRGHTS TO GUILT (0)
PRELIS
   /VARIABLES=HUMRGHTS TO GUILT (OR)
   /MATRIX = OUT ('PRL_MTRX OUTPUT')
```

Of course, once such an active SPSS system file has been created, PRELIS could be used more than once on this file—for instance, to investigate the effect of a variable transformation, or the dichotomizing of variables. No output file will be created in this example. Note that the VARIABLES subcommand does three things here. It establishes the scale type, it selects the variables in the active file, and it also reorders them. The TEMPORARY command has the effect that the recoded and transformed variables will be restored to their original values immediately after the next procedure—in this case the second PRELIS command—such that other possibilities could be explored in the same session with another PRELIS command.

```
TITLE "POLYCHORIC, POLYSERIAL AND PRODUCT-MOMENT CORRELATIONS"
DATA LIST FILE='PRL_RAW DATA' FREE
   /1 CONTIN1 ORDINAL1 ORDINAL2 ORDINAL3 CONTIN2 ORDINAL4
MISSING VALUES CONTIN1 TO ORDINAL4 (-9)
PRELIS
   /VARIABLES=CONTIN1 CONTIN2 (CO) ORDINAL1 TO ORDINAL3 (OR)
   /MISSING=PAIRWISE EXCLUDE
   /MATRIX=NONE
   /TYPE=POLY
TITLE "AFTER RECODINGS AND TRANSFORMATION"
TEMPORARY
COMPUTE CONTIN1 = LN(3 + CONTIN1)
RECODE ORDINAL1 (1 THRU 5=0) (6 THRU 7=1)
RECODE ORDINAL2 (1 THRU 2=0) (3 THRU 5=1)
PRELIS
   /VARIABLES=CONTIN1 CONTIN2 (CO) ORDINAL1 TO ORDINAL3 (OR)
```

```
    /MISSING=PAIRWISE EXCLUDE
    /MATRIX=NONE
    /TYPE=POLY
```

In the following example a LISREL analysis will be done on raw data that are read from an external file, specified on the RA subcommand. The labels for the variables are also read from an external file, specified on the LA subcommand. In this case, the LISREL program will compute a covariance matrix (the default) from the raw input data, and will use it as the matrix to be analyzed.

```
LISREL
    / "KLEIN'S MODEL I ESTIMATED BY IV AND ULS"
    / DA NO=21 NI=15
    / LA FI='LS7_LAB INPUT'
    / RA FI='LS7_DAT INPUT'
    / MO NY=8 NX=7 BE=FU GA=FI PS=FI
    / OU UL
```

The alternative method starts from an SPSS system file containing the raw data.

```
GET FILE='LS7PROB DATA'
LISREL
    / "KLEIN'S MODEL I ESTIMATED BY IV AND ULS"
    / DA NI=15
    / MO NY=8 NX=7 BE=FU GA=FI PS=FI
    / OU UL
```

Only the numeric values in the file "LS7PROB DATA" will be used. The RA and LA subcommands are not needed. In both cases, if the NO keyword has not been set on the DA subcommand, LISREL will compute it from the data file. Note that the number of variables NI has to be set, even if the input comes from the active file.

Instead of raw data, the user will oftentimes only have access to summary data (covariances, correlations, standard deviations, etc.) for analysis. The next example shows how to create a matrix system file as the active file, containing correlations and standard deviations. All data in such a matrix system file should be valid; missing values are not allowed. The command MCONVERT transforms this into a covariance matrix, which will then be analyzed by LISREL. The number of cases (267) is also obtained from the SPSS active system file.

```
MATRIX DATA VARIABLES=GESCOM_A GESCOM_B CONWOR_A CONWOR_B
     HIDPAT_A HIDPAT_B THIROUND THIBLUE VOCABU_A VOCABU_B
     /CONTENTS=CORR STDDEV /N=267
BEGIN DATA
 1
 .74 1
 .33 .42 1
 .34 .39 .65 1
 .26 .21 .15 .18 1
 .23 .24 .22 .21 .77 1
 .15 .12 .14 .11 .17 .20 1
 .14 .14 .14 .15 .06 .09 .42 1
-.04 -.03 .09 .16 .06 .09 .19 .21 1
 .02 .02 .10 .23 .04 .07 .09 .21 .72 1
 2.42 2.80 3.40 3.19 1.94 1.79 5.63 3.10 3.05 2.25
```

```
END DATA
MCONVERT
LISREL
   /"EXAMPLE 6.2: SECOND-ORDER FACTOR ANALYSIS"
   /DA NI=10
   /MO NY=10 NE=5 NK=2 GA=FI PH=ST PS=DI
   /LE
   /GESCOM CONWOR HIDPAT THINGS VOCABU
   /LK
   /SPEEDCLO VOCABUL
   /VA 1 LY 1 1 LY 2 1 LY 3 2 LY 4 2  LY 5 3 LY 6 3
         LY 7 4 LY 9 5 LY 10 5
   /FR LY 8 4 GA 1 1 GA 2 1 GA 3 1 GA 4 2 GA 5 2
   /ST 1 ALL
   /OU SE TV SS NS
```

The command **MCONVERT** was used because the summary data available were not of the type that we wanted to analyze. Although LISREL can do quite a few transformations, this one is not possible when a matrix system file is the data source (and, of course, not needed). To summarize the transformation possibilities, we have to distinguish among the various ways that data can be input. The example above belongs to the recommended situation where a matrix system file is active, the vertical arrow that points to LISREL in Figure A–1. The other situation, the three horizontal arrows, will be discussed first.

The three horizontal arrows that point to LISREL in Figure A–1 are the endpoints of the following three paths. Raw data are read inline (included with the Command File) or from an external (ASCII) file; the active file is an SPSS system file containing raw data; summary data are read inline or from an external file. Figure A–2 gives an overview of the possible matrices that can be analyzed, given the type of input data and one of those three input modes. Thus, when a covariance matrix (CM) and a vector of means (ME) are available (and the data are either inline or read from an external file), LISREL could be instructed to analyze either that covariance matrix (CM), the matrix of moments about zero (MM), or the augmented moment matrix (AM). It should be pointed out that the LISREL program assumes default values for means (zero) and standard deviations (one), thus it is always possible to analyze any type of matrix (AM, CM, KM, MM), regardless of available input. Note that we use the LISREL keywords for raw data (RA), covariance matrix (CM), correlation matrix (KM), standard deviations (SD), means (ME), matrix of moments (MM), and augmented moment matrix (AM).

Figure A–2. Alternative data input and possible LISREL analysis.

INPUT (available)	MATRIX TO BE ANALYZED (possible)			
RA	AM	CM	KM	MM
CM + SD		CM	KM	
KM + SD		CM	KM	
MM + ME	AM	CM		MM
CM + ME	AM	CM		MM
KM + SD + ME	AM	CM	KM	MM

The analysis of an augmented moment matrix is still a possibility in LISREL 7 to maintain compatibility with LISREL 6. Instead of analyzing moment structures, it is now possible to specify mean structures directly (intercept terms in the equations and/or mean values of latent variables in the model): see Chapter 10 of *LISREL 7: A Guide to the Program and Applications.*

It is recommended to create a matrix system file with the summary data and let LISREL obtain *all* its data information from there. *It is not possible to combine these alternatives.* For example, having LISREL read correlations from a matrix system file, and read standard deviations inline, instructing LISREL to create a covariance matrix to be analyzed, does not work. All summary data have to follow the same path (not counting the special summary data that PRELIS may generate, asymptotic variances and covariances).

The SPSS LISREL interface will recognize five different rowtypes in the matrix system file: CORR, COV, MOMNT, MEAN, and N (see also p. C–5, below); and it will generate the corresponding subcommands (KM, CM, MM, ME, and the NO keyword on the DA subcommand). It does not recognize the rowtype for standard deviations. As pointed out above, when you need to transform correlations into covariances, and vice versa, use the command MCONVERT before starting LISREL. The reader might observe that there is only one rowtype for correlations (CORR), while PRELIS can produce various types of correlations. In the SPSS system all these different correlations will be passed to LISREL with the KM subcommand, which is generated by the SPSS LISREL interface. However, the user informs the LISREL program about the type of correlation matrix by setting the keyword MA (matrix to be analyzed) on the DA subcommand to either KM, OM, or PM, for product-moment, optimal score based, or polychoric and polyserial correlations, respectively.

Because LISREL accepts the rowtype MOMNT (which is produced by PRELIS) but the MATRIX DATA command has no such keyword, the following should be done in the unlikely event that moments about zero are the available summary data.

```
MATRIX DATA VAR = VAR1 TO VAR4 / CONTENTS = MAT MEAN / N=100
BEGIN DATA
. . .
END DATA
RECODE ROWTYPE_ ('MAT' = 'MOMNT')
LISREL
   / . . .
```

The rowtype MAT has been chosen here (for a generic square matrix), but because it will be recoded to MOMNT anyway, CORR, COV, or PROX (the other keywords for a square matrix of coefficients) will work as well.

With these two considerations in mind, we are now able to produce the figure that will present the same overview as Figure A–2 for matrix system file input, the default mode of data input in LISREL. You could use Figure A–3 for answering the question “If I want to do a LISREL analysis on a correlation matrix, what type of data do I need, and which steps are needed before the actual LISREL analysis?” The answer is: read a correlation matrix into a matrix system file, or read a covariance matrix into a matrix system file and use the command MCONVERT next, before LISREL. Or, when raw data are available, an SPSS system file could be used, or the PRELIS command. “All possibilities” in Figure A–3 has been given because PRELIS offers more possibilities than just AM, CM, KM, and MM.

Figure A–3. Recommended data input and possible LISREL analysis.

DATA (available)	SPSS COMMANDS before LISREL	LISREL ANALYSIS (possible)			
Raw data	PRELIS	All possibilities			
Raw data	(Active system file)	AM	CM	KM	MM
CM	MATRIX DATA		CM		
KM	MATRIX DATA			KM	
MM	MATRIX DATA, RECODE				MM
CM+SD	MATRIX DATA, MCONVERT			KM	
KM+SD	MATRIX DATA, MCONVERT		CM		
CM+ME	MATRIX DATA	AM	CM		MM
MM+ME	MATRIX DATA, RECODE	AM	CM		MM
KM+SD+ME	MATRIX DATA, MCONVERT	AM	CM		MM

Stacked Problems, Multi-Sample Analysis, and Split Files

A special way of using PRELIS and LISREL involves the use of the "split-file" possibilities in the SPSS system. In the following example an SPSS system file with raw data also includes a variable GROUP that flags one of several groups in the data. The first PRELIS command results in a separate analysis for each group. Next, the split-file condition of the active file is switched off, causing a PRELIS analysis for all groups combined.

```
GET FILE='MULTIGRP DATA'
SORT CASES BY GROUP
SPLIT FILE BY GROUP
PRELIS
   / ...
   / MATRIX OUT ('MULTIGRP MATRIX')
   / ...
SPLIT FILE OFF
PRELIS
   / ...
```

The file "MULTIGRP MATRIX" is a split matrix system file, consisting of separate matrices for each value of the split variable "GROUP." It may be used subsequently to drive multi-group or stacked problem analysis in LISREL.

As in this example, analyzing several problems with LISREL in one session is also best done by stacking LISREL commands. In LISREL, however, there is another option. A set of subcommands may be repeated under the same LISREL command, which implies, of course, that a fatal error in an earlier set will prevent further sets from being executed. A subcommand set is defined as everything between and including the DA and OU subcommands, which is why the DA subcommand should always come first (except for possible title lines) and the OU subcommand last. The MATRIX subcommand that was added in the SPSS implementation, if used, may precede the first subcommand set or be part of it. As it is not allowed to use both this MATRIX subcommand and native data input subcommands, like SD, it is not allowed to mix the two over several subcommand sets that are stacked under one LISREL command.

In multi-group analysis, the NG keyword on the DA subcommand specifies the number of groups, and the same number of subcommands sets should follow the LISREL command. See Chapter 9 in *LISREL 7: A Guide to the Program and Applications* for multi-group or multi-sample analysis.

Here is an overview of the ways that split-files, stacked subcommand sets, and multi-group analysis relate within the SPSS system ($N \neq M$, $N > 1$, $M > 1$).

Figure A–4. Split-files and stacked subcommand sets in LISREL.

Number of subcommand sets	Number of split groups	Result
1	1	One single group analysis
1	N	Identical single group analyses on N different data sets
N	1	N different single group analyses on the same data set
N	N	One multi-group analysis
N	M	Fatal error

The NG keyword on the DA subcommand will automatically be set by the SPSS LISREL interface. It should equal 1 in all cases except the "one multi-group analysis" case, where it should equal N. If the user sets this value differently, a fatal error results. The only possibility not mentioned is N different single group analyses with N different data sets. This is not possible with a split (matrix) system file, since N subcommand sets with N split groups and the NG keyword set to 1 results in a fatal error. It can be done by stacking `LISREL` commands in one session, each one preceded by a replacement of the active (matrix) system file, or using the subcommand `MATRIX IN (file)`, where the filename will change.

The following example uses a split matrix system file with two groups and results in two different multi-group analyses, because each LISREL Command File has two subcommand sets.

```
TITLE "FROM 'LISREL 7: A GUIDE TO THE PROGRAM AND APPLICATIONS'"
MATRIX DATA    /* NOTE THAT SPSS VAR NAMES DO NOT ALLOW HYPHENS
   VARIABLES=STATUS ROWTYPE_ READ_GR5 WRIT_GR5
                             READ_GR7 WRIT_GR7
   / SPL=STATUS / FORMAT=LIST LOWER DIAGONAL
BEGIN DATA
1 COV      281.349
1 COV      184.219 182.821
1 COV      216.739 171.699 283.289
1 COV      198.376 153.201 208.837 246.069
1 N        373     373     373     373
2 COV      174.485
2 COV      134.468 161.869
2 COV      129.840 118.836 228.449
2 COV      102.194  97.767 136.058 180.460
2 N        249     249     249     249
END DATA
LIST
LISREL
   /"EXAMPLE 9.1A: HYPOTHESIS A (BOYS ACADEMIC)"
   /"TESTING EQUALITY OF FACTOR STRUCTURES.     "
   /DA NI=4
   /MO NX=4 NK=4 LX=ID TD=ZE
```

```
   /OU
   /"EXAMPLE 9.1A: HYPOTHESIS A (BOYS NON-ACADEMIC)"
   /DA
   /MO PH=IN
   /OU
LISREL
   /"EXAMPLE 9.1B: HYPOTHESIS B (BOYS ACADEMIC)"
   /"TESTING EQUALITY OF FACTOR STRUCTURES.      "
   /DA NI=4 NG=2
   /MO NX=4 NK=2
   /FR LX 2 1 LX 4 2
   /VA 1 LX 1 1 LX 3 2
   /OU
   /"EXAMPLE 9.1B: HYPOTHESIS B (BOYS NON-ACADEMIC)"
   /DA
   /MO LX=PS
   /OU
```

The LIST command displays the newly created matrix system file in the output so it may be compared with the "matrix to be analyzed" that is part of the LISREL output to make sure that the input for LISREL is indeed as expected.

Additional Options

Some consequences of the PRELIS and LISREL implementation in the SPSS system insofar as it affects the user are discussed in this section. Note that the stand-alone versions may speak of "commands" or "command lines," whereas the SPSS system calls the same level of program instructions "subcommands."

In both procedures, slashes are used as the delimiters that separate subcommands. As a consequence, a slash in a LISREL Command File now may have one of three different meanings, dependent on context. Most often, it means the start of a new subcommand. If there are two consecutive slashes, at most separated by blanks or return characters, the first slash signals the (premature) end of data to LISREL. For instance, the SE subcommand in the following Command File selects a subset of the twelve (NI=12) variables in the input file. After the SE subcommand, the program expects a list of variables. Not all of the original variables are in the list. The slash signals the end; no more variable names will follow. It is an end-of-data slash because the next relevant character is also a slash, signaling the start of a new subcommand.

```
LISREL
  / DA NI=12 ...
  / ...
  / SE
  / VAR1 VAR2 VAR4 VAR5 VAR10 VAR11 /
  / MO ...
  / ...
```

Finally, a third and more exceptional occurrence of the slash in a LISREL Command File is within a FORTRAN format statement, where it means to skip the rest of that record and proceed to the next record. The context of this slash, the format statement, can be defined as "the slash is somewhere between two parentheses," since that is a requirement for FORTRAN format statements.

Command lines in native LISREL may be continued on the next physical line by using a continuation mark (the letter C). Otherwise, the return character at the end of the physical line would signal end-of-command to the program. On the other hand, several commands may be given on the same physical line by using the semicolon as the delimiter. In SPSS syntax the slash is the subcommand delimiter, and the return character has no special meaning for subcommands. Therefore, subcommands may extend over several physical lines (as long as they are indented at least one column) and more than one subcommand could be given on the same physical line. Still, it is possible to use both the continuation mark and the semicolon within an SPSS LISREL Command File, a consequence of the decision to maintain the native syntax as much as possible. But it is strongly recommended to use the slash throughout.

Whenever the implementation of LISREL in the SPSS system results in alternate possibilities and a preferred way exists, we will mention it. The section "Data Input" above has several such instances. For example, it is recommended to create an SPSS system file or matrix system file containing the data to be analyzed, instead of using the LISREL possibilities of reading raw or summary data directly from an external file, or inline, within the Command File. Then, the dictionary of the system file will be used to pass the variable names to the LISREL procedure. And naturally, the user has to obey the SPSS syntax rules when naming the variables. Thus, a hyphen in a variable name is not allowed. However, in native LISREL (where variable names are called "labels") such a practice is allowed ("VAR-1" and "KSI-1" are indeed default variable names in native LISREL), and the LISREL 7 textbook has several examples. It is even possible in native LISREL to have blanks in variable names if those names are protected with apostrophes. If a user opts to enter data directly in a LISREL analysis, including variable names (instead of using the program defaults), the correct way of naming two variables `VAR-1` and `VAR 2` would be (see the LISREL Subcommand Reference for the `LA` subcommand):

```
/LA
/'VAR-1' "'VAR 2'"
```

In SPSS LISREL this extra layer of protective quote marks is needed, because the SPSS system strips off one layer before it passes character strings on to the LISREL program. Again, the use of SPSS system files avoids those problems.

In native LISREL, data could be read either in fixed or in free format. In the latter case no format statement is needed, but the user might indicate free format with a line containing only an asterisk (*). If a user would quickly adapt a native LISREL Command File, containing such an asterisk, by inserting a space and a slash in front of each record (and, of course, preceding everything with the procedure command `LISREL`), the slash asterisk combination (/*) now signals the start of a comment instead of free format. Since the asterisk is not really needed to signal free format, nothing unexpected will happen. But if the same user now decides to shorten this Command File somewhat by combining short subcommands on the same physical line, the /* could create a problem: if subcommands follow on the same line, they will be seen as the comment by the SPSS system, and are not passed on to the LISREL program. Therefore, do not use the asterisk to indicate data in free format. Better yet, use SPSS system files, and the problem does not exist.

Some options of the PRELIS stand-alone version were not included in the SPSS version because the SPSS system offers the same possibilities elsewhere, such as a logarithmic or a power transformation for continuous variables to approximate normal distribution characteristics for those variables, or the regression of every variable in the dataset on all other variables to explore the possibilities of structural relationships in the data. Case weighting is now accomplished with the SPSS **WEIGHT** command (only integers are allowed). In SPSS PRELIS, things like the title line and the width of the display file come from the SPSS **TITLE** command and the SPSS **SET WIDTH** command, while in SPSS LISREL they are part of the subcommand syntax. Both programs can produce output 80 or 132 columns wide.

A final problem that needs mentioning is that errors and warnings produced by the PRELIS program do sometimes refer to the native syntax. The first Appendix gives the SPSS PRELIS user an interpretation in terms of the SPSS PRELIS syntax.

PRELIS
User's Guide

Contents

PRELIS User's Guide

Users of LISREL need to know the characteristics of their data well so they can avoid any problems that might arise. To help LISREL users become aware of these problems and avoid mistakes, a new program, PRELIS, has been developed.

It is particularly important to know the scale type of each variable, the distribution of each variable, the distribution of the variables jointly, and the distribution of missing values over variables and cases.

When some or all of the variables are ordinal or censored, it is essential to choose the right type of correlations to analyze. Failure to do so can lead to considerable bias in estimated LISREL parameters and other quantities. PRELIS can help with these considerations and with others summarized briefly below and described in detail on the following pages.

Data

PRELIS can read grouped data and patterned data where each case carries a weight.

PRELIS does a fair amount of data screening. Although other programs may provide more detailed data screening, no other program is available that can compute all the kinds of correlations and other moments for ordinal and censored variables.

The program can be used to take a first, quick look at data from questionnaires in surveys.

Variables

The scale type of each variable may be declared as ordinal, censored (see page B–2), or continuous. Groups of variables (including all variables) of the same scale type may be declared collectively. Ordinal variables may have up to 15 categories.

The program can estimate correlations between censored variables and ordinal or continuous variables.

Continuous variables may be transformed using any one of a large family of transformations. Ordinal variables may be recoded or transformed to normal scores, or they may first be recoded and then transformed to normal scores. Maximum and/or minimum values of censored variables may be transformed to normal scores.

PRELIS can compute Mardia's measure of relative multivariate kurtosis.

Correlations

PRELIS replaces that part of LISREL 6 which computes polychoric and polyserial correlations, and it does them much better, much faster, and with more informative output.

PRELIS computes various types of correlation coefficients: product-moment (Pearson) based on raw scores, product-moment based on normal or optimal scores (the latter are sometimes called canonical correlations), polychoric (including tetrachoric), and polyserial (including biserial).

For each polychoric and polyserial correlation, the program provides a test of the model underlying the computation of this correlation.

PRELIS can compute estimates of the asymptotic variances and covariances of estimated product-moment correlations, polychoric correlations, and polyserial correlations; these can be used with WLS (Weighted Least Squares) in LISREL 7.

Matrices

PRELIS computes the appropriate moment matrix (moment matrix about zero, covariance matrix, or correlation matrix) for input to LISREL, depending on the type of variables in the data.

Moment matrices may be computed using either pairwise deletion or listwise deletion.

PRELIS produces an estimate of the asymptotic (large sample) covariance matrix of the estimated sample variances and covariances under arbitrary non-normal distributions (see Browne, 1982, 1984). This can be used to compute a weight matrix for WLS (Weighted Least Squares, equivalent to Browne's ADF) in LISREL 7.

PRELIS may be used to compute a diagonal matrix consisting of estimates of the asymptotic variances of estimated variances, covariances, or correlations. These diagonal matrices can be used with DWLS (Diagonally Weighted Least Squares) in LISREL 7.

Output

PRELIS printed output is compact, yet it contains detailed information about all univariate and bivariate sample distributions.

The program writes the requested moment matrix onto an SPSS matrix system file that can be used by LISREL. Requested asymptotic covariance matrices will be saved in a format that can be read directly by LISREL 7.

Three Types of Variables

PRELIS can deal with three types of variables: continuous, ordinal and censored.

Continuous variable: observations are assumed to come from an interval or a ratio scale and to have metric properties. Means, variances, and higher moments of these variables will be computed in the usual way.

Ordinal variable: observations are assumed to represent responses to a set of ordered categories, such as a five-category Likert scale. Here it is only assumed that a person who responds in one category has more of a characteristic than a person who responds in a lower category. For each ordinal variable x, it is assumed that there is a latent continuous variable ξ that is normally distributed with mean zero and unit variance. The assumption of normality is not testable given only x; but for each pair of variables where x is involved, PRELIS attempts a test of the assumption of bivariate normality.

Assuming that there are k categories on x, we write $x = i$ to mean that x belongs to category i. The actual score values in the data may be arbitrary and are irrelevant as long as the ordinal information is retained. That is, low scores correspond to low-order categories of x which are associated with smaller values of ξ, and high scores correspond to high-order categories which are associated with larger values of ξ.

The connection between x and ξ is that $x = \xi$ is equivalent to $\alpha_{i-1} < \xi \leq \alpha_i$, where $\alpha_0 = -\infty$, $\alpha_1 < \alpha_2 < \cdots < \alpha_{k-1}$, and $\alpha_k = +\infty$, are parameters called threshold values. If there are k categories, there are $k - 1$ unknown thresholds.

Censored variable: x represents a latent variable ξ observed on an interval scale above a threshold value A. Below A, the value $x = A$ is observed:

$$x = \xi \quad \text{if} \quad \xi > A\,,$$
$$x = A \quad \text{if} \quad \xi \le A\,.$$

The value A is known and is equal to the smallest observed value of x. The latent variable ξ is assumed to be normally distributed with unknown mean μ and standard deviation σ, which are estimated by the maximum likelihood method.

The censored variable just defined will be said to be ***censored below***. PRELIS can also deal with variables that are ***censored above***:

$$x = \xi \quad \text{if} \quad \xi < B\,,$$
$$x = B \quad \text{if} \quad \xi \ge B\,.$$

Variables that are censored ***both above and below*** are also handled by PRELIS.

Censored variables have a high concentration of cases at the lower or upper end of the distribution. The classical example of this is in Tobit analysis where, for example, x = the price of an automobile purchased in the last year, with $x = 0$ if no car was purchased. Here ξ may represent a propensity to consume capital goods. Other examples may be x = number of crimes committed or x = number of days unemployed. Test scores that have a "floor" or a "ceiling"—a large proportion of cases with no items or with all items correct—are censored variables. Attitude questions where a large fraction of the population is expected to have the lowest or highest score or category may also be considered censored variables.

A key concept in the way PRELIS treats ordinal and censored variables is the use of normal scores.

For an ordinal variable, let n_j be the number of cases in the j-th category. The threshold values are estimated from the (marginal) distribution of each variable as

$$\hat{\alpha}_i = \Phi^{-1}\Big(\sum_{j=1}^{i} n_j/N\Big), \qquad i = 1,\,2,\,\ldots,\,k-1$$

where Φ^{-1} is the inverse standard normal distribution function, and N is the total number of real observations on the ordinal variable. The ***normal score*** z_i corresponding to $x = i$ is the mean of ξ in the interval $\alpha_{i-1} < \xi \le \alpha_i$, which is (see Johnson & Kotz, 1970, pp. 81–82)

$$z_i = \frac{\phi(\alpha_{i-1}) - \phi(\alpha_i)}{\Phi(\alpha_i) - \Phi(\alpha_{i-1})}\,,$$

where ϕ and Φ are the standard normal density and distribution function, respectively. This normal score can be estimated as

$$\hat{z}_i = (N/n_i)[\phi(\hat{\alpha}_{i-1}) - \phi(\hat{\alpha}_i)]\,.$$

As can be readily verified, the weighted mean of the normal scores is 0.

For a variable censored below A, PRELIS uses the normal score associated with the interval $\xi \le A$, which is

$$\hat{z}_A = \hat{\mu} - \frac{\phi[(A-\hat{\mu})/\hat{\sigma}]}{\Phi[(A-\hat{\mu})/\hat{\sigma}]}\hat{\sigma}\,,$$

where $\hat{\mu}$ and $\hat{\sigma}$ are the maximum likelihood estimates of μ and σ.

For a variable censored above B, the normal score associated with the interval $\xi \geq B$ is

$$\hat{z}_B = \hat{\mu} + \frac{\phi[(B - \hat{\mu})/\hat{\sigma}]}{\Phi[(B - \hat{\mu})/\hat{\sigma}]}\hat{\sigma} .$$

Choosing the Type of Correlation Matrix to Analyze

When one or more of the variables to be analyzed in LISREL is ordinal, it is important to choose the right type of moment matrix to analyze. Because ordinal variables do not have an origin or unit of measurement, the only meaningful moment matrices, when all variables are ordinal, are correlation matrices. PRELIS provides four choices:

- **CORRELATION (continuous).** A matrix of product-moment (Pearson) correlations based on raw scores; *i.e.*, with scores 1, 2, 3, ... on ordinal variables treated as if they come from interval-scaled variables. This is produced with the `TYPE=CORRELATION` specification in SPSS PRELIS when *all* variables are declared *continuous.*
- **CORRELATION (ordinal).** A matrix of product-moment (Pearson) correlations with observations on ordinal variables replaced by normal scores determined from the marginal distributions. This is produced with the `TYPE=CORRELATION` specification in SPSS PRELIS when *ordinal* variables are declared *ordinal.*
- **OPTIMAL.** A matrix of product-moment (Pearson) correlations with observations on ordinal variables replaced by optimal scores determined for each pair. This is produced with the `TYPE=OPTIMAL` specification in SPSS PRELIS when *ordinal* variables are declared *ordinal.*
- **POLYCHOR.** A matrix of polychoric correlations. This is produced with the `TYPE=POLYCHOR` specification in SPSS PRELIS when *ordinal* variables are declared *ordinal.*

The first three of these correlation types correspond to some sort of scoring system for the categories and the product-moment correlation computed for this scoring system. For example, OPTIMAL chooses scores for the categories that will maximize the correlation. The polychoric correlation (POLYCHOR), on the other hand, is not a correlation between two sets of scores, but is, rather, an estimate of the correlation in the latent bivariate normal distribution representing the two ordinal variables.

Jöreskog & Sörbom (1988) report two Monte Carlo studies to investigate which of these correlations is "best." The first involved only ordinal variables; the second involved both ordinal and continuous variables. These experiments included two correlations—Spearman's rank correlation and Kendall's tau-b—that are not included as options in PRELIS because of their poor results in the study.

The general conclusions they draw from the first type of Monte Carlo experiments, in which the distributions of two ordinal variables were varied, are as follows:

- All correlations are biased downwards, but the bias for POLYCHOR is small and negligible for moderate sample sizes.
- POLYCHOR, CORRELATION (ordinal), and OPTIMAL do not appear to be sensitive to the shape of the marginal distributions.

- POLYCHOR is generally the best estimator, but the relative performances of CORRELATION (ordinal) and OPTIMAL are improved as the number of categories increases, especially in moderate samples.

- POLYCHOR is almost always the best correlation in each sample in the sense of being closest to the true ρ. OPTIMAL is mostly second, and CORRELATION (ordinal) is third.

- Only POLYCHOR appears to be a consistent estimator of ρ. Although variances of all the other correlations are small, their biases do not become small when the sample size increases.

In the second study six variables were generated from a multivariate normal distribution with a covariance matrix constructed such that a factor analysis model with two correlated factors and a clear simple structure was satisfied exactly (see Jöreskog, 1979). Next, four of the variables were transformed into ordinal variables, one was made skewed, one U-shaped, the third symmetrical, while the fourth was dichotomous. The other two variables were left unchanged. Twenty percent of the 400 observations generated were randomly set to missing.

PRELIS was used to compute the four types of correlation matrices using both pairwise and listwise deletion. This yielded eight estimated correlation matrices. Each was compared to the true correlation matrix.

Each of the eight correlation matrices was further analyzed with LISREL to fit a restricted (confirmatory) factor analysis model with two correlated factors. The factor loading matrix had three fixed zeros in each column (see Jöreskog, 1979). The maximum likelihood (ML) method was used in LISREL to fit the model, even though there was no theoretical justification for using ML in this case.

- In terms of bias and mean square error, there seems to be a clear trend: CORRELATION (continuous) and CORRELATION (ordinal) are most biased and have the largest mean square error; OPTIMAL performs somewhat better; and POLYCHOR is least biased and has the smallest mean square error. This holds for both pairwise and listwise deletion.

- In this case, pairwise deletion gave better results than listwise deletion. This is undoubtedly because 20 percent of the observations were missing at random, reducing the effective sample size under listwise deletion to only 102, while the pairwise sample sizes varied from 240 to 328.

- The correlations were mostly underestimated. This resulted in underestimates of factor loadings and in overestimates of unique variances.

- All eight correlation matrices generated by PRELIS were positive-definite. The ML method gave good results even when some of the variables are ordinal. This demonstrates that, although normal-theory chi-square values and standard errors are not valid, the ML method may still be used to fit the model to the data.

- The measures of overall fit that LISREL computes—chi-square, adjusted goodness of fit index (AGFI), and root mean squared residual (RMSR)—behave quite normally.

- This was a single case study from which very well-established conclusions cannot be drawn. To obtain clearer and more exact results, a full-scale Monte Carlo study should be undertaken.

Six Types of Moment Matrices

Some of the various types of moment matrices that the program can compute are defined in this section and illustrated by means of a small dataset.

The basis of analysis in PRELIS is a data matrix **Z** with N rows and k columns:

$$\mathbf{Z} = \begin{bmatrix} z_{11} & z_{12} & \cdots & z_{1k} \\ z_{21} & z_{22} & \cdots & z_{2k} \\ \vdots & \vdots & \ddots & \vdots \\ z_{N1} & z_{N2} & \cdots & z_{Nk} \end{bmatrix}$$

The columns represent *variables*. The rows represent statistical units (individuals, companies, regions, occasions, etc.) on which the variables have been observed or measured.

In this manual we shall refer to a row of the data matrix as a *case* on which the variables have been observed or measured. A case may be a *single observation* (as when the row characterizes an individual) or a *multiple case* (as when the row characterizes a whole group of individuals with identical responses to the variables). When a row of the data matrix represents a pattern of observations, the row carries a weight equal to the number of individuals having the same responses.

Each element $z_{\alpha i}$ is a numeric value. For continuous variables, these values represent observations or measurements on an interval scale or ratio scale. For ordinal variables the values represent arbitrary score values, such as 1,2,3,4,5 of a 5-category Likert scale. Still other values in the data matrix may represent missing observations.

An example of such a data matrix is shown below. It consists of 12 cases on four variables. (The sample size 12 is far too small to be useful in any LISREL model. Nevertheless, this small dataset will be used here for illustrative purposes, as it is possible to check most of the computations by hand.)

Case	Var 1	Var 2	Var 3	Var 4
1	1	3	−0.7	−0.4
2	2	4	2.3	1.6
3	3	3	1.2	1.7
4	1	−9	−0.4	−0.3
5	3	2	−1.2	−0.7
6	2	1	−9.0	1.2
7	2	1	0.8	0.3
8	3	3	1.6	1.5
9	1	2	−0.9	−9.0
10	1	4	−0.8	−0.8
11	1	1	0.7	0.8
12	2	2	1.1	1.3

Variables 1 and 2 are assumed to be ordinal variables. The three entries of "−9" are specified by the user to represent missing observations. PRELIS can handle missing data using either pairwise or listwise deletion. Both methods are discussed next.

Pairwise Deletion

To begin with, we shall pretend that all four variables are continuous. Let n_{ij} be the number of cases having real observations on both variables i and j (the effective sample sizes under *pairwise deletion*). The n_{ij} form a symmetric matrix N of order $k \times k$. For the data of our small illustrative example the matrix N is:

$$\mathbf{N} = \begin{bmatrix} 12 & & & \\ 11 & 11 & & \\ 11 & 10 & 11 & \\ 11 & 10 & 10 & 11 \end{bmatrix} .$$

Some of the moment matrices can now be defined.

The moment matrix (TYPE=MOMENT) is defined to be the symmetric matrix $\mathbf{M} = (m_{ij})$ whose elements are

$$m_{ij} = (1/n_{ij}) \sum_{\alpha} z_{\alpha i} z_{\alpha j} ,$$

where the summation is over all cases with real observations on both variables i and j. This definition applies when $i = j$ as well. The elements of M represent moments about zero or mean squares and products. For the small dataset,

$$\mathbf{M} = \begin{bmatrix} 4.000 & & & \\ 4.545 & 6.727 & & \\ 1.009 & 1.180 & 1.379 & \\ 1.418 & 1.510 & 1.223 & 1.176 \end{bmatrix} .$$

The covariance matrix (TYPE=COVARIANCE) is defined as the symmetric matrix $\mathbf{S} = (s_{ij})$ whose elements are

$$s_{ij} = [1/(n_{ij} - 1)] \sum_{\alpha} (z_{\alpha i} - \bar{z}_i)(z_{\alpha j} - \bar{z}_j) ,$$

where

$$\bar{z}_i = (1/n_{ij}) \sum_{\alpha} z_{\alpha i} , \qquad \bar{z}_j = (1/n_{ij}) \sum_{\alpha} z_{\alpha j} .$$

As before, the three sums are based on all non-missing observations on both variables i and j. By this definition, a different mean z_i generally will be used when the variance s_{ii} is computed instead of when the covariance s_{ij} is computed. The mean that will be used depends upon which cases were deleted. For our small data matrix,

$$\mathbf{S} = \begin{bmatrix} 0.697 & & & \\ 0.036 & 1.255 & & \\ 0.437 & 0.172 & 1.393 & \\ 0.376 & -0.056 & 1.103 & 0.945 \end{bmatrix} .$$

Here, for example, $s_{21} = 0.036$ is based on 11 cases, $s_{11} = 0.697$ is based on 12 cases, and $s_{22} = 1.255$ is based on 11 cases.

The correlation matrix (TYPE=CORRELATION) is the matrix $\mathbf{R} = (r_{ij})$, whose elements are

$$r_{ij} = s_{ij}/d_i d_j ,$$

where

$$d_i^2 = [1/(n_{ij} - 1)] \sum_{\alpha} (z_{\alpha i} - \bar{z}_i)^2 , \qquad d_j^2 = [1/(n_{ij} - 1)] \sum_{\alpha} (z_{\alpha j} - \bar{z}_j)^2 .$$

Both sums are over all real observations on both variables i and j. Note that d_i^2 is not necessarily the same as s_{ii}. When computing r_{ij} $(i \neq j)$, d_i^2 is based on n_{ij} cases whereas s_{ii} is based on n_{ii} cases. For the small dataset,

$$\mathbf{R} = \begin{bmatrix} 1.000 & & & \\ 0.039 & 1.000 & & \\ 0.424 & 0.131 & 1.000 & \\ 0.466 & -0.048 & 0.946 & 1.000 \end{bmatrix}.$$

The three matrices **M**, **S**, and **R** were computed without distinguishing between ordinal and continuous variables. Data values on ordinal variables were treated as if they came from interval scales. However, by declaring the first two variables to be ordinal, other types of correlation matrices can be obtained.

When some of the variables are declared ordinal, the arbitrary score values of these variables are replaced by their corresponding normal scores before **M**, **S**, or **R** is computed.

For variable 2 in our small dataset, the computation of the normal scores is as follows:

Category	Marginal Frequency	Upper Threshold	Normal Score
1	3	−0.605	−1.218
2	3	0.114	−0.235
3	3	0.908	0.485
4	2	$+\infty$	1.452

The weighted mean of these normal scores is zero and the weighted variance is 0.954—smaller than 1 because it is the between-category variance of ξ.

The within-category variance is $1 - 0.954 = 0.046$, and the total variance of ξ is 1. The resulting moment matrices are:

$$\mathbf{M} = \begin{bmatrix} 0.785 & & & \\ 0.020 & 0.868 & & \\ 0.447 & 0.160 & 1.379 & \\ 0.435 & -0.042 & 1.223 & 1.176 \end{bmatrix}.$$

$$\mathbf{S} = \begin{bmatrix} 0.856 & & & \\ 0.022 & 0.954 & & \\ 0.499 & 0.123 & 1.393 & \\ 0.426 & -0.064 & 1.103 & 0.945 \end{bmatrix}.$$

$$\mathbf{R} = \begin{bmatrix} 1.000 & & & \\ 0.024 & 1.000 & & \\ 0.437 & 0.108 & 1.000 & \\ 0.477 & -0.064 & 0.946 & 1.000 \end{bmatrix}.$$

Besides the correlation matrix `TYPE=CORRELATION` described above, there are two other types of correlation matrices, `TYPE=OPTIMAL` and `TYPE= POLYCHOR`, which can be used when some or all of the variables are ordinal. These correlation matrices consist of three different types of correlations. For each pair of variables one of the following three alternatives will occur:

1) When ***both variables are continuous*** (interval scaled), the product-moment correlation is computed from all complete pairs of observations. This correlation is the same in `TYPE=OPTIMAL` and `TYPE=POLYCHOR`.

2) When ***both variables are ordinal***, a contingency table is obtained from which the correlation is computed. Under **TYPE=OPTIMAL**, this correlation is the product-moment correlation of optimal scores or the *canonical correlation* (see Kendall & Stuart, 1961, pp. 568–573). Under **TYPE=POLY- CHOR**, this correlation is the maximum likelihood estimate of the *polychoric correlation*, where an underlying bivariate normal distribution is assumed.

3) When ***one variable is ordinal and the other is continuous***, the program obtains the mean and variance of the continuous variable for each category of the ordinal variable and uses these summary statistics to compute the *polyserial correlation* (assuming again an underlying bivariate normal distribution). Under **TYPE=OPTIMAL** a simple consistent estimator will be used, but under **TYPE=POLYCHOR** a maximum likelihood estimator will be used (see Jöreskog, 1986).

The end product of this procedure is a correlation matrix for all the variables, where each correlation has been estimated separately. Although it is rare in practice, experience indicates that such a correlation matrix sometimes fails to be positive-definite. When a correlation matrix which is not positive-definite is to be used to estimate a LISREL model, the ML or GLS method cannot be used. In LISREL 6, the ULS method must be used instead. In LISREL 7, WLS and DWLS may also be used. Furthermore, even if the matrix of correlations is positive-definite, these correlations are unlikely to behave like ordinary sample moments, not even asymptotically. So if one uses the ML or GLS methods for fitting the model, one should not rely on the normal theory standard errors and chi-square goodness-of-fit measures supplied by LISREL. Correct large sample standard errors and chi-square values can be obtained with WLS in LISREL 7.

When both variables are ordinal, information provided in the data may be represented as a contingency table. For the illustrative data, the contingency table for variables 1 and 2 is:

	VAR 2				
VAR 1	1	2	3	4	Marginal
1	1	1	1	1	4
2	2	1	0	1	4
3	0	1	2	0	3
Marginal	3	3	3	2	11

Let x and y be two ordinal variables with p and q categories, respectively. Let n_{ij} $(i = 1, 2, \ldots, p,\ j = 1, 2, \ldots, q)$ be the corresponding frequencies in the contingency table.

Optimal scores for x and y are defined as two sets of ordered score values that maximize the product-moment correlations, subject to the constraints that the means are 0 and the variances are 1 (see Kendall & Stuart, 1961, pp. 568–573). The product-moment correlation of these optimal scores, sometimes called *canonical correlation*, is obtained as the second largest eigenvalue of a symmetric matrix formed from the elements of the contingency table.

The *polychoric correlation* is not a correlation between a pair of score values. Rather it is an estimate of the correlation between two latent variables η and ξ underlying y and x, where η and ξ are assumed to have a bivariate normal distribution. For our illustrative data the polychoric correlation between variables 1 and 2 is estimated as 0.030.

This latent correlation can be estimated by the maximum likelihood method based on the multinomial distribution of the cell frequencies in the contingency table. The estimation procedure follows Olsson (1979), but the computational algorithm has been considerably improved since LISREL 6. The algorithm in PRELIS is often 20 times faster than that of LISREL 6.

Next consider the third case, when one variable is ordinal and one variable is continuous. In our small dataset there will be four such pairs of variables: (3,1), (3,2), (4,1), and (4,2). In the illustration below, we use the pair (3,1). Let x be an ordinal variable with p categories, and let y be a continuous variable. As before, let n_i be the number of cases in category i of x. Corresponding to these cases there will be n_i values on y denoted

$$y_{i1}, y_{i2}, \ldots, y_{in_i}.$$

Let $\bar{y}_i$ and s_i^2 be the mean and unbiased variance of these values. (If $n_i = 1$, the variance is zero and this category cannot be used in the computations. However, the required correlation can still be computed, provided there are at least 2 categories with $n_i > 1$.) For the pair (3,1) these summary statistics are:

Category	Number of Observations	Mean	Standard Deviation
1	5	−0.756	0.653
2	3	1.064	0.794
3	3	0.197	1.514

The *polyserial correlation* is the correlation between the observed variable y and a latent variable ξ, where y and ξ are assumed to have a bivariate normal distribution. This can be estimated by the maximum likelihood method as described by Jöreskog (1986). Under **TYPE=OPTIMAL**, Jöreskog's Method 1 is used; under **TYPE=POLYCHOR**, Jöreskog's Method 5 is used.

For our illustrative data, the correlation matrices obtained under the **TYPE=OPTIMAL** and **TYPE=POLYCHOR** options are:

$$\mathbf{O} = \begin{bmatrix} 1.000 & & & \\ 0.676 & 1.000 & & \\ 0.503 & 0.121 & 1.000 & \\ 0.528 & -0.074 & 0.946 & 1.000 \end{bmatrix}.$$

$$\mathbf{P} = \begin{bmatrix} 1.000 & & & \\ 0.030 & 1.000 & & \\ 0.478 & 0.122 & 1.000 & \\ 0.536 & -0.071 & 0.946 & 1.000 \end{bmatrix}.$$

Listwise Deletion

So far we have dealt with pairwise deletion. With *listwise deletion*, all cases with missing observations are deleted first so that the data matrix reduces effectively to a matrix without missing observations. All the definitions above still apply. The main difference is that under listwise deletion, all computations are based on the same cases. This will guarantee that all the matrices obtained under **TYPE=MOMENT**, **TYPE=COVARIANCE**, and **TYPE=CORRELATION** are non-negative-definite. Correlation matrices obtained under **TYPE=OPTIMAL** and **TYPE=POLYCHOR** still cannot be guaranteed to be non-negative-definite, as they may consist of different types of correlations.

Producing Weight Matrices and Fit Functions

As one of its options, PRELIS produces the *asymptotic covariance matrix* of estimated covariances and correlations. This section explains what this matrix is and how it can be used to produce *weight matrices* for certain fit functions in LISREL 7.

A general family of fit functions for analysis of covariance structures may be written (see, *e.g.*, Browne, 1984)

$$\begin{aligned} F(\boldsymbol{\theta}) &= (\mathbf{s}-\boldsymbol{\sigma})'\mathbf{W}^{-1}(\mathbf{s}-\boldsymbol{\sigma}) \\ &= \sum_{g=1}^{k}\sum_{h=1}^{g}\sum_{i=1}^{k}\sum_{j=1}^{i} w^{gh,ij}(s_{gh}-\sigma_{gh})(s_{ij}-\sigma_{ij}) , \end{aligned} \qquad (1.1)$$

where

$$\mathbf{s}' = (s_{11}, s_{21}, s_{22}, s_{31}, \ldots, s_{kk})$$

is a vector of the elements in the lower half, including the diagonal, of the covariance matrix **S** of order $k \times k$ used to fit the model to the data;

$$\boldsymbol{\sigma}' = (\sigma_{11}, \sigma_{21}, \sigma_{22}, \sigma_{31}, \ldots, \sigma_{kk})$$

is the vector of corresponding elements of $\Sigma(\boldsymbol{\theta})$ reproduced from the model parameters $\boldsymbol{\theta}$; and $w^{gh,ij}$ is a typical element of a positive-definite matrix $\mathbf{W}^{-1}$ of order $p \times p$, where $p = k(k+1)/2$. In most cases, the elements of $\mathbf{W}^{-1}$ are obtained by inverting a matrix $\mathbf{W}$ whose typical element is denoted $w_{gh,ij}$. The usual way of choosing $\mathbf{W}$ in weighted least squares is to let $w_{gh,ij}$ be a consistent estimate of the asymptotic covariance between s_{gh} and s_{ij} but, in principle, any positive-definite matrix $\mathbf{W}$ may be used. To estimate the model parameters $\boldsymbol{\theta}$, the fit function is minimized with respect to $\boldsymbol{\theta}$.

Under very general assumptions, if the model holds in the population and if the sample variances and covariances in **S** converge in probability to the corresponding elements in the population covariance matrix $\boldsymbol{\Sigma}$ as the sample size increases, any such fit function will give a consistent estimator of $\boldsymbol{\theta}$. In practice, numerical results obtained by one fit function are often close enough to the results that would be obtained by another fit function, to allow the same substantive interpretation.

Further assumptions must be made, however, if one needs an asymptotically correct chi-square test of goodness-of-fit and asymptotically correct standard errors of parameter estimates.

"Classical" theory for covariance structures (see, *e.g.*, Browne, 1974, or Jöreskog, 1981), assumes that the asymptotic variances and covariances of the elements of **S** are of the form

$$\text{ACov}(s_{gh}, s_{ij}) = (1/N)(\sigma_{gi}\sigma_{hj} + \sigma_{gj}\sigma_{hi}) . \qquad (1.2)$$

where N is the total sample size. This holds, in particular, if the observed variables have a multivariate normal distribution, or if **S** has a Wishart distribution. The GLS (Generalized Least Squares) and ML (Maximum Likelihood) methods available in LISREL 6 and their chi-square values and standard errors are based on these assumptions. The GLS method corresponds to using a matrix $\mathbf{W}$ in (1.1) whose general element is

$$w_{gh,ij} = (1/N)(s_{gi}s_{hj} + s_{gj}s_{hi}) . \qquad (1.3)$$

The fit function for ML is not of the form (1.1) but may be shown to be equivalent to using a $\mathbf{W}$ of the form (1.3), with $\mathbf{s}$ replaced by an estimate of $\boldsymbol{\sigma}$ which is updated in each iteration.

In recent fundamental work by Browne (1982, 1984), this classical theory for covariance structures has been generalized to any multivariate distribution for continuous variables satisfying very mild assumptions. This approach uses a **W** matrix with typical element

$$w_{gh,ij} = m_{ghij} - s_{gh}s_{ij} \ , \qquad (1.4)$$

where

$$m_{ghij} = (1/N)\sum_{\alpha=1}^{N}(z_{\alpha g} - \bar{z}_g)(z_{\alpha h} - \bar{z}_h)(z_{\alpha i} - \bar{z}_i)(z_{\alpha j} - \bar{z}_j)$$

are the fourth-order central moments. Using such a **W** in (1.1) gives what Browne calls "asymptotically distribution free best GLS estimators" for which correct asymptotic chi-squares and standard errors may be obtained. As shown by Browne, this **W** matrix also may be used to compute correct asymptotic chi-squares and standard errors for estimates that have been obtained by the classical ML and GLS methods. When **W** is defined by (1.4), we call the fit function WLS (Weighted Least Squares) to distinguish it from GLS where **W** is defined by (1.3). WLS and GLS are different forms of weighted least squares: WLS is asymptotically distribution free, while GLS is based on normal theory.

While WLS is attractive in theory, it presents several difficulties in practical applications. First, the matrix **W** is of order $p \times p$ and has $p(p+1)/2$ distinct elements. This increases rapidly with k, demanding large amounts of computer memory when k is at all large. For example, when $k = 20$, **W** has 22155 distinct elements. Second, to estimate moments of fourth order with reasonable precision requires very large samples. Third, when there are missing observations in the data, different moments involved in (1.4) may be based on different numbers of cases unless listwise deletion is used. When pairwise deletion is used, it is not clear how to deal with this problem.

Finally, Browne's (1984) development is a theory for sample *covariance* matrices for continuous variables. In practice, however, correlation matrices often are analyzed; *i.e.*, covariance matrices scaled by stochastic standard deviations. The elements of such a correlation matrix do not have asymptotic variances and covariances of the form (1.2), even if **S** has a Wishart distribution. In PRELIS, an estimate of the asymptotic covariance matrix of the estimated *correlations* can also be obtained under the same general assumptions of non-normality. This approach can be used when some or all of the variables are ordinal or censored, after the raw scores are replaced by normal scores. PRELIS can also compute estimates of the asymptotic variances and covariances of estimated polychoric and polyserial correlations. This approach is similar to that of Muthén (1984), but the PRELIS estimates are much simpler and faster to compute.

A correlation matrix estimated in PRELIS with the **TYPE=CORRELATION** or **TYPE=POLYCHOR** options has $q = k(k-1)/2$ estimated correlations and, as a consequence, the asymptotic covariance matrix of these correlations is of order $q \times q$. To obtain the weight matrix to be used in LISREL 7, this covariance matrix must be inverted. The inversion is not performed by PRELIS but is part of LISREL 7. The asymptotic covariance matrix of estimated coefficients obtained by PRELIS may be saved in a file that can be read directly by LISREL 7.

To sum up: whenever possible in PRELIS, an estimate of the asymptotic covariance matrix of the elements of the estimated moment matrix is provided. Currently, such asymptotic covariance matrices are available for sample covariance matrices and matrices of product-moment (Pearson), polychoric, and/or polyserial correlations. Asymptotic covariance matrices are not yet available for moments about zero, augmented moment matrices, or correlation matrices based on optimal scores.

Computation of asymptotic covariance matrices of estimated coefficients is very time-consuming and demands large amounts of memory when the number of variables is large. An alternative approach, which may be used even when the number of variables is large, is to compute only the asymptotic variances of the estimated coefficients. Let w_{gh} be an estimate of the asymptotic variance of s_{gh}. These estimates may be used with a fit function of the form

$$F(\theta) = \sum_{g=1}^{k} \sum_{h=1}^{g} (1/w_{gh})(s_{gh} - \sigma_{gh})^2 \tag{1.5}$$

This corresponds to using a diagonal weight matrix $\mathbf{W}^{-1}$ in (1.1). In LISREL 7 this is called DWLS (Diagonally Weighted Least Squares). This does not lead to asymptotically efficient estimates of model parameters but is offered as a compromise between unweighted least squares (ULS) and fully weighted least squares (WLS). DWLS can also be used when correlation matrices (**TYPE=CORRELATION** or **TYPE=POLYCHOR**) are analyzed.

PRELIS
Subcommand Reference

- *Introduction*
- *Subcommands*
- *PRELIS Syntax*

Contents

Introduction

This section of the Subcommand Reference is an introduction that provides general information about the PRELIS procedure and its subcommands. After this introduction, a detailed section titled "Subcommands" describes the subcommands individually in alphabetical order. At the end of the Subcommand Reference is a complete syntax chart. See "PRELIS and LISREL within SPSS" in Part A for additional information.

Syntax Notation

Like other SPSS commands, a PRELIS command begins in column 1 and is followed by subcommands and keywords in free format. A command, including its subcommands with related specifications, can continue for as many lines as needed. Indent all continuation lines at least one column.

Space is usually required to separate the elements of a command from one another. You can add space or break lines at any point where a single blank can occur, including around special delimiters such as slashes, parentheses, or equals signs. To break a literal (an item in apostrophes) across two lines, place each line in apostrophes but join them with a + sign. The maximum length of an input line, usually 80 characters, can vary based on the type of computer and operating system. If you go beyond column 72, remember to include the UNNUMBERED command.

The syntax for each PRELIS subcommand is presented in the Subcommands section. The syntax diagrams use a shorthand style that follows these rules:

- Elements printed in upper case are subcommands or keywords.
- Elements in lower case describe items you should provide.
- Subcommands and keywords can be truncated up to the first three characters.
- Equals signs are optional.
- Parentheses ( ) are part of the syntax and must be entered exactly as shown.
- Slashes are required between subcommands.
- Blanks or commas must separate keywords, names, labels, and numbers.
- Elements enclosed in square brackets [ ] are optional. The brackets are not part of the syntax.

- Braces {} are not part of the syntax either. They indicate a choice among the elements they enclose. Use only one alternative from a list in braces.
- Ellipses ... also are not part of the syntax. They indicate the possibility of repeating an element or an entire sequence of elements.
- Default options are in **boldface** type and starred (**). A default is the option SPSS assumes is in effect if you do not explicitly request an alternative.

When the user repeats subcommands or keywords, a warning will be issued and the latter subcommand or keyword will be used.

Single Group Analysis

Unlike LISREL, which can analyze data from several groups simultaneously, PRELIS can only analyze data from one group at a time, because it reads each data set twice: first, for univariate screening; then, to compute the requested correlations, covariances, or moments.

Raw data may be available from several groups. If each group is to be analyzed separately, the data must be read from separate files. If the groups will be jointly analyzed, all data must first be combined into one file. Of course, SPSS users may keep their data organized in one system file and use the SPLIT FILE command to do analyses for separate groups (see p. A–9). The following combination of separate group analysis and joint analysis may occasionally be useful.

Restrictions

PRELIS has the following built-in restrictions:

- Polychoric and polyserial correlations will not be computed unless the pairwise sample size is at least 20.
- Asymptotic variances and covariances of estimated variances, covariances, and correlations will not be computed unless the listwise sample size is at least 200 if $k < 12$, and at least $1.5k(k+1)$ if $k \geq 12$, where k is the number of variables.
- The number of categories in an ordinal variable can be no more than 15. If a variable has more than 15 distinct values, not counting missing values, it will be treated as continuous.

General Operations

A PRELIS command without any following specifications results in a product-moment correlation matrix of all the numeric variables in the SPSS active system file. It will be printed and written to a matrix system file that replaces the active file. All variables are treated as continuous and the computation is under listwise deletion, both-user missing values and system-missing values being excluded. The display file will be 80 characters wide, unless the width has been set to 132 characters or more. The title is taken from the SPSS run title.

Logarithmic and power transformations of variables, recoding of variables, regression, and case selection, all options of stand-alone PRELIS, should now be done with the equivalent SPSS commands. Case weighting is accomplished with the SPSS WEIGHT command.

Split groups in the active file will be processed independently and the resulting matrix system file will be split accordingly. The matrix of asymptotic variances or covariances will be written in a format that LISREL can read. It is not an SPSS system file.

Subcommands

CRITERIA

```
/ CRITERIA = [ ASIZE ( { 200 **          } ) ] [ DEFAULT ]
                       { 1.5k(k+1)  ** }
                       { n               }
```

Overview Asymptotic variances and covariances of estimated variances, covariances, and correlations will not be computed unless the listwise sample size is at least 200 if $k < 12$, and at least $1.5k(k+1)$ if $k \geq 12$, where k is the number of variables. If the asymptotic variances and/or covariances are really needed, the best procedure would be to add more cases to the analysis. However, the CRITERIA subcommand allows you to relax the restriction by specifying a smaller value than required. *This possibility should be used with very careful attention, because results produced in small samples may not be at all reliable.*

Operations The default minimum sample size depends on the number of variables as defined above. If the computation of asymptotic variances and/or covariances is requested (see the WRITE and PRINT subcommands), then the user will be warned when the sample size is too small. To change the sample size restriction, allowing computation of the asymptotic (co)variances, specify a smaller size between parentheses after the ASIZE keyword on the CRITERIA subcommand. The DEFAULT keyword may be used to reset the CRITERIA subcommand to its default values, a feature that is useful when SPSS is used interactively.

MATRIX

```
/ MATRIX = { NONE                 }
           { OUT ( {*    } ) ** }
                   {file}
```

Overview The analysis matrix produced by PRELIS will be written to the active matrix system file, by default, ready to be read by a subsequent LISREL command. The MATRIX subcommand allows for alternate actions.

Operations The OUT specification designates where to write the analysis matrix. If no file name is provided, a default file name will be used. An asterisk (*) in place of a file name indicates that the matrix is to be written to the active file, in this case a matrix system file. In the absence of a MATRIX subcommand the analysis matrix will be written to the active file by default. The keyword NONE means that no matrix system file will be generated.

The following is a summary of matrix file structures. The rowtypes created in the analysis matrix are dependent on the specification on the TYPE subcommand. The first part of the analysis matrix is a square symmetric matrix of correlations, covariances, or moments. When AUGMENTED has been specified on the TYPE subcommand, this square matrix is followed by a row of means. All matrices terminate with a row (for listwise deletion of missing values) or a matrix (for pairwise deletion of missing values) of N's. With pairwise deletion, the SPSS LISREL interface will set the NO keyword on the DA subcommand equal to the minimum value found in the matrix of N's.

TYPE	ROWTYPE	FORM
AUGMENTED	MOMNT	Moment matrix
	MEAN	Row of means
	N	Row or square symmetric matrix with the number of cases
CORRELATION	CORR	Matrix of product-moment correlations
	N	Row or square symmetric matrix with the number of cases
COVARIANCE	COV	Covariance matrix
	N	Row or square symmetric matrix with the number of cases
MOMENT	MOMNT	Moment matrix
	N	Row or square symmetric matrix with the number of cases
OPTIMAL	CORR	Matrix of optimal correlations
	N	Row or square symmetric matrix with the number of cases
POLYCHOR	CORR	Matrix of product-moment, polyserial, and/or polychoric correlations
	N	Row or square symmetric matrix with the number of cases

MAXCAT

```
/ MAXCAT = { 0 ** }
           { n    }
```

Overview

To specify the maximum number of categories for ordinal variables. This subcommand functions as a global declaration for all variables. It is overridden by the scale type declarations for specific variables on the **VARIABLES** subcommand.

Operations

- The *maximum* value accepted for n is 15. Values greater than 15 will generate a warning and be reset to 15. Non-integer values will generate a warning and be truncated, while non-numeric and negative values will cause the program to stop.
- If the subcommand **MAXCAT** is not used, or if it is specified as 0 or 1, then all variables will be regarded as continuous, *except* any variables that are explicitly declared as ordinal on the **VARIABLES** subcommand.
- Variables that are declared to be censored (on the **VARIABLES** subcommand) will be treated as continuous, even if the **MAXCAT** specification and their number of distinct values would result in an ordinal scale type.

MISSING

```
/ MISSING = [ { LISTWISE ** } ] [ { EXCLUDE ** } ]
              { PAIRWISE    }     { INCLUDE    }
```

Overview The MISSING subcommand determines the treatment of cases with user-missing values. System-missing values are never considered valid.

Operations LISTWISE and PAIRWISE are mutually exclusive, as are EXCLUDE and INCLUDE. LISTWISE and EXCLUDE are the defaults.

Listwise deletion means that computations will be based only on cases with real observations on *all* variables. Pairwise deletion implies that computations will be based on all cases with real observations on *both* variables. See page B–7 through B–10 of the PRELIS User's Guide above for a discussion of pairwise and listwise deletion.

When EXCLUDE has been specified, user-missing values are invalid. To include them in the analysis, use the INCLUDE keyword.

PRINT

```
/ PRINT = [ { NONE ** } ] [ KURTOSIS ]
            { ACOV    }
            { AVAR    }

          [ XBIVARIATE ] [ XTEST ]
```

Overview To obtain *additional* output or to suppress part of the default output. The asymptotic variances, the asymptotic covariances, and the relative multivariate kurtosis are possible additional output. The bivariate tables and the test statistics may be excluded from the standard output.

Operations

- The default is NONE (no *optional* printout).
- The keyword ACOV causes an asymptotic covariance matrix to be printed. The keyword AVAR causes an asymptotic variance matrix to be printed. If ACOV or AVAR is requested, it should also be specified on the WRITE subcommand. However, if omitted, the program sets this automatically, issuing a warning.
- The asymptotic covariances and variances (ACOV or AVAR) can only be estimated under listwise deletion and are not available for TYPE = AUGMENTED, TYPE = MOMENT, or TYPE = OPTIMAL (see page B–13). Another restriction is the sample size, which should be sufficiently large (see the CRITERIA subcommand).
- A kurtosis measure (see Mardia, 1970) will be printed when the keyword KURTOSIS has been specified. It is available only when a covariance matrix under listwise deletion has been requested, and when the covariance matrix is positive-definite.
- By specifying the XBIVARIATE keyword the bivariate tables for ordinal variables will *not* be printed in the output. Likewise, the test statistics for polychoric and polyserial correlations will *not* be printed when the keyword XTEST has been given.

TYPE

```
/ TYPE = { NONE             }
         { AUGMENTED        }
         { CORRELATION **   }
         { COVARIANCE       }
         { MOMENT           }
         { OPTIMAL          }
         { POLYCHOR         }
```

Overview This subcommand specifies the type of moment matrix (see part B) to be estimated. The default is **CORRELATION**, generating a product-moment (Pearsonian) correlation matrix. A correlation matrix based on optimal scores is generated by specifying the keyword **OPTIMAL**, while **POLYCHOR** produces a matrix of product-moment, polychoric, and/or polyserial correlations, dependent on the scale type of the variables. **COVARIANCE** results in a covariance matrix being generated, **MOMENT** produces a matrix of moments about zero, while **AUGMENTED**, finally, generates an augmented moment matrix, which implies that a row of means will follow the matrix of moments about zero. See the **MATRIX** subcommand for an overview of the matrix file structures that may be selected with the **TYPE** subcommand. The keyword **NONE** causes PRELIS only to screen the raw data.

Operations For polychoric and polyserial correlations the sample size should be at least 20, else the program will issue an error and stop. Another fatal error arises when the contingency table for two ordinal variables has only one row or only one column. This means that one variable has fewer than two actual categories for the other, given the data, and the polychoric correlation cannot be computed. For a polyserial correlation (between an ordinal and a continuous variable), there should be at least two categories of the ordinal variable for which the within variance is positive. If there is only a single case in a category, or all the values for the continuous variable in a category of the ordinal variable are equal, the variance will be zero. Such a category cannot be used in the computation of the polyserial correlation and the program will issue a warning. If this results in less than two categories for the ordinal variable, the polyserial correlation cannot be computed at all and the program will stop with an error message.

VARIABLES

```
/ [ VARIABLES = ] var-name [ ( { CONTINUOUS   } ) ] ...
                               { ORDINAL      }
                               { CABOVE       }
                               { CBELOW       }
                               { CENSORED     }
```

Overview

Use this subcommand

- if you do not want all the numeric variables in the active file (the default) to enter the analysis,
- if you want the variables (or a subset) in a different order,
- if you want to override the global scale-type declaration on the MAXCAT subcommand for specific variables,
- or if you have censored variables in your analysis.

See the PRELIS User's Guide (Part B, page B–2) for an explanation of the different scale types.

Operations

- The variable list is not required. The default is all the numeric variables in the active file.
- The "VARIABLES" subcommand name is optional. However, when it is deleted (including the equals sign), the list of variables should follow immediately after the PRELIS command.
- The scale type (CONTINUOUS, ORDINAL, CABOVE, CBELOW, or CENSORED), given between parentheses immediately after each variable name, may be truncated to the first *two* characters (CO, OR, CA, CB, and CE, respectively). Omitting the closing (right) parenthesis will generate a warning, but processing will continue. The opening (left) parenthesis is a required part of the syntax.
- There is no default scale type. The specification on the MAXCAT subcommand or its default sets the scale type for all variables as either ordinal or continuous (interval scaled). This may be changed with the specific OR and CO declarations on the VARIABLES subcommand. Note that a variable with more than 15 distinct values, not counting missing values, will be treated as continuous, despite an OR specification. The user will be warned when an ordinal variable has more than 15 distinct values.
- Censored variables must be explicitly declared on this subcommand with the scale types CA, CB, or CE. After the maximum and/or minimum value of the censored variable has been replaced by its corresponding normal score, the variable is treated as continuous.
- Scale type refers to *all* variables preceding it that are not otherwise specified. For instance, in the next specification VAR2 and VAR3 are also declared to be ordinal.

```
/VARIABLES VAR1 (CO) VAR2 VAR3 VAR4 (OR)
```

This implies that as soon as a specification of the scale type for one variable is needed, all the variables that will enter the analysis have to be listed, even if all the numeric variables of the default file are being used.

WRITE

```
/ WRITE = { NONE **     }
          { ACOV file }
          { AVAR file }
```

Overview The optional **WRITE** subcommand is used to save the asymptotic (co)variance matrix of the estimated variances, covariances, or correlations in a file for subsequent use with the (D)WLS method in LISREL.

Operations **NONE** is the default. The filename clause of the **WRITE** subcommand designates where the variance or covariance matrix is to be written. If this clause is omitted, the user will be warned and the default filename will be used. But only a covariance matrix may be written to the default file, so **AVAR**, if specified without a filename, will be overridden by **ACOV**. These output files are not written as SPSS matrix system files. Their only use is as input files for the LISREL 7 command, so they are written in a format that can be read directly by the LISREL program.

The asymptotic covariances and variances (**ACOV** or **AVAR**) can only be estimated under listwise deletion and are not available for **TYPE = AUGMENTED**, **TYPE = MOMENT**, or **TYPE = OPTIMAL** (see page B–13). Another restriction is the sample size, which should be sufficiently large (see the **CRITERIA** subcommand).

When **ACOV** or **AVAR** is specified on the **PRINT** subcommand, the **WRITE** subcommand is required with the same specification. If omitted, a warning will be issued and the program sets the **WRITE** subcommand.

PRELIS Syntax

Syntax Chart

```
PRELIS

    [ / [VARIABLES =] [ var-name [({ CONTINUOUS })] [ ... ] ]
                                  { ORDINAL    }
                                  { CABOVE     }
                                  { CBELOW     }
                                  { CENSORED   }

    [ / MISSING    = [{ LISTWISE ** }] [{ EXCLUDE ** }] ]
                      { PAIRWISE    }   { INCLUDE    }

    [ / MAXCAT     =  { 0 ** } ]
                      { n    }

    [ / TYPE       =  { NONE           } ]
                      { AUGMENTED      }
                      { CORRELATION ** }
                      { COVARIANCE     }
                      { MOMENT         }
                      { OPTIMAL        }
                      { POLYCHOR       }

    [ / MATRIX     =  { OUT ( { *    } )** }
                              { file }
                      { NONE               } ]

    [ / WRITE      =  { NONE **     } ]
                      { ACOV [file] }
                      { AVAR [file] }

    [ / PRINT      = [{ NONE ** }] [ KURTOSIS ]
                      { ACOV    }
                      { AVAR    }

                     [ XBIVARIATE ] [ XTEST ] ]

    [ / CRITERIA   = [ ASIZE ({ 200 **        }) ] [ DEFAULT ] ]
                              { 1.5k(k+1) ** }
                              { n            }
```

Syntax Notation

- Subcommand order is unimportant. However, if the optional **VARIABLES** subcommand name is omitted (including the optional equals sign), the list of variables should immediately follow the **PRELIS** command. The order shown is more or less the logical order.
- The variable list is not required. The default is all the numeric variables in the active file.
- Scale types are **ORDINAL**, **CONTINUOUS**, **CENSORED**, **CABOVE**, and **CBELOW**. These keywords may be truncated up to the first two characters.
- Equals signs are optional. Other special delimiters (( ) and /) must be entered exactly as shown.
- Uppercase elements are subcommands or keywords. They must be entered as they appear, or may be truncated up to the first three characters.
- Lowercase elements describe items to be filled in by the user.
- Slashes are required between subcommands. A slash will be tolerated immediately following the command name, *i.e.*, before the first subcommand. A slash following the last subcommand is optional.
- Use blanks or commas to separate keywords, names, labels and numbers.
- Square brackets [ ] enclose optional specifications not necessary for the correct completion of the command. The brackets should not be coded.
- Braces {} enclose alternative specifications. One (and only one) of these specifications must be entered in order to complete the specifications correctly. The braces themselves should not be coded.
- Ellipses ... indicate the possibility of repeating an element or an entire sequence of elements.
- **Boldface**, starred (**) entries denote default specifications. The double asterisks should not be coded; only a single asterisk may be part of the syntax.

LISREL 7
Subcommand Reference

- *Introduction*
- *Subcommands*
- *LISREL Syntax*

Contents

Introduction

This section of the Subcommand Reference is an introduction that provides general information about the LISREL procedure and its subcommands. After this introduction, a detailed section titled "Subcommands" describes the subcommands individually and in alphabetical order. The Subcommand Reference ends with a complete description of the LISREL syntax. See "PRELIS and LISREL within SPSS" in Part A for additional information.

Syntax Notation

Like other SPSS commands, a **LISREL** command begins in column 1 and is followed by subcommands and keywords in free format. A command, including its subcommands with related specifications, can continue for as many lines as needed. Indent all continuation lines at least one column.

Space is usually required to separate the elements of a command from one another. You can add space or break lines at any point where a single blank can occur, including around special delimiters such as slashes, parentheses, or equals signs. The maximum length of an input line, usually 80 characters, can vary based on the type of computer and operating system. If you go beyond column 72, remember to include the **UNNUMBERED** command.

The syntax diagrams in this LISREL Subcommand Reference use a shorthand style that follows these rules:

- Elements printed in upper case are subcommands or keywords.
- Elements in lower case describe items you should provide.
- LISREL subcommands and keywords can be truncated up to the first two characters. There are three exceptions. The subcommand **MATRIX**, its keyword **NONE**, and the option **ALL** on the **ST** and **VA** subcommands have *three* significant characters.
- Special delimiters (**( )**, =, **,**, and /) must be entered exactly as shown.
- Slashes are required between subcommands.
- Blanks or commas must separate keywords, names, labels, and numbers.
- Elements enclosed in square brackets [ ] are optional. The brackets are not part of the syntax.
- Braces {} are not part of the syntax either. They indicate a choice among the elements they enclose. Use only one alternative from a list in braces.

- Ellipses **. . .** also are not part of the syntax. They indicate the possibility of repeating an element or an entire sequence of elements.
- Default options are in **boldface** type, and starred (**). A default is the option SPSS assumes is in effect if you do not explicitly request an alternative.

Except for raw data in the active file and summary data in the active file or in a matrix system file, none of the files referred to are SPSS system files. They will be referred to as "external files," and will be mostly plain ASCII type files.

Preparing the LISREL Command File

Execution of LISREL problems is controlled by a Command File describing three phases of processing:

1) data input; 2) model construction; 3) output of results.

Subcommands

A typical LISREL subcommand consists of a two-letter subcommand name, one or more option names, and one or more keywords followed by specified values.[1]The order of options and keywords is immaterial. In the subcommand descriptions to follow, a subcommand line is represented in the form:

$$
\begin{array}{lllllll}
/\,\text{Name} & [\text{Keyword}_1 = a] & \{\text{Keyword}_{2'} = b'\,\} & \ldots & [\text{Option}_1] & \{\text{Option}_{2'}\,\} & \ldots \\
 & & \{\text{Keyword}_{2''} = b''\} & & & \{\text{Option}_{2''}\} & \\
 & & \vdots & & & \vdots &
\end{array}
$$

Only one of the keywords or options enclosed in braces may be selected. If a keyword has several alternative values (in braces), only one value may be given. The square brackets denote that the keyword or option is not required to complete the subcommand. Of course, the subcommand itself may be optional. The equals sign is required in keywords. Options and keywords may be separated by commas or blanks. Blanks on either side of an equals sign are permitted. The subcommand line ends when the next subcommand (or a new command) starts. Although it is not required, it is recommended to end each subcommand with a carriage return, such that the next subcommand starts on a new line. All examples in this manual follow that strategy, making it easier to check the Command File for correct order and completeness. As in all SPSS commands, subcommands should not use the first column of a new line; in other words, they are indented. In the textbook *LISREL 7: A Guide to the Program and Applications* you will find several examples with more than one subcommand on the same physical line, separated by a semicolon. This is also allowed in SPSS LISREL, but not recommended. Because the slash in SPSS syntax has the function of separating subcommands, the function of the LISREL semicolon (as well as the return character) for delimiting subcommands becomes obsolete. Another practice one can find in the textbook is the use of a C in place of an option or keyword as a continuation mark. This informs the program that the particular subcommand will be continued on the next physical line. For SPSS LISREL users this practice has also become obsolete, because the return character does not separate

[1]Messages (errors or warnings) in the program output still use the term "parameter" instead of "keyword" or "option." To avoid confusion with model parameters, this manual uses the new terminology.

subcommands in the SPSS syntax. The user may continue a subcommand over several physical lines, if needed (each time skipping the first column).

Significant characters. Only the first two characters are significant in subcommand names, options, keywords and character keyword values. Any additional characters up to the first blank, comma, slash or equals sign will be ignored. The use of the semicolon, another delimiter allowed in native LISREL syntax, would also have that effect, but its use is unnecessary and not recommended in SPSS LISREL. Thus,

DA, DATA, DAta, and data

are all equivalent. There are a few exceptions to this rule. The option **ALL** on the **VA** and **ST** subcommands has three significant characters; that is, it may not be abbreviated to **AL**. Likewise, the **MATRIX** subcommand, which has been specifically added to the LISREL syntax for SPSS use, and its option **NONE** have three significant characters.

Detail Lines

Apart from typical LISREL subcommands (see Table 1 below for an overview), the LISREL Command File may contain two other types of "subcommands." So-called *detail lines*: *format statements* and *data lines*. The latter are either character strings (for labels) or numbers. In SPSS LISREL all these lines have to start with a forward slash to delineate them from each other, and therefore have the appearance of subcommands, although they are, of course, not proper subcommands.

The **RA** subcommand, for example, may be followed by the data for the problem if desired. Large data sets are usually placed in a separate file, however. In general it is recommended that all data be read from external files, not from the Command File. In that way the program can better detect errors in the data. SPSS users will generally start the LISREL procedure with their input data in the active file, which reduces the need for detail lines enormously. See the section "Data Input" in Part A for more details.

FORTRAN Format Statements

When data (labels, raw data, summary statistics, patterns or parameter matrix values) are used in fixed format, a FORTRAN format statement is needed to instruct the program how to read the data. The general form of such a statement is

$$(rCw) \text{ or } (rCw.d),$$

where:

- r Repeat count; if omitted, 1 is assumed.
- C Format code:
  - A Code for character values (used in **LA**, **LK** and **LE** subcommands)
  - I Code for integer values (used in the **PA** subcommand)
  - F Code for real numbers (used in **RA**, **CM**, **ME**, **SD**, etc., subcommands)
- w Field width, or number of columns.
- d Number of decimal places (for F-format).

The format statement should be enclosed in parentheses. Blanks within the statement are ignored: $(\ r\ C\ w\ .\ d\ )$ is acceptable.

Examples:

The labels HEIGHT, WEIGHT, AGE and IQ could be read in fixed format as:

```
/(A6,A6,A3,A2)
/HEIGHTWEIGHTAGEIQ
```

Or, with the same result, as:

```
/(4A6)
/HEIGHTWEIGHT   AGE    IQ
```

Note that the first method lets the repeat count default to 1, and that it describes several different fields, separated by commas, with one statement.

The following example shows three ways to read five integers, with the same result:

```
/(5I1)
/12345
/(5I2)
/ 1 2 3 4 5
/(I1,I2,3I3)
/1 2  3  4  5
```

The F-format requires the number of decimal places in the field description, so if there are none (and eight columns), specify (F8.0); (F8) is not allowed. However, if a data value contains a decimal point, then this overrides the location of the decimal point as specified by the general field description. If the general field description is given by (F8.5), then 12345678 would result in the real number +123.45678, but the decimal point in −1234.56 would not change. Just a decimal point, or only blanks, will result in the value zero. The plus sign is optional.

Use the X format descriptor to skip over unneeded variables. For instance, (F7.4,8X,2F3.2) informs the program that the data file has 21 columns per record. The first value can be found in the first seven columns (and there are four decimal places), then eight columns should be skipped, and a second and third value are in columns 16–21, both occupying three columns (with two decimal places).

Another possibility is the use of the tabulator format descriptor T, followed by a column number *n*. For instance, (1F8.5, T60, 2F5.1) describes three data fields; in columns 1–8, with five decimal digits, next in columns 61–65 and 66–70, both with one decimal digit. If the number *n* is smaller than the current column position, left-tabbing results. Left tabs should be used cautiously. No problems are known when data records are shorter than 256 columns.

A forward slash (/) in an F-format means "skip the rest of this line and continue on the next line." Thus, (F10.3//5F10.3) instructs the program to read the first variable on the first line, then to skip the remaining variables on that line, to skip the following line completely, and to read five variables on the third line. As will be clear from the examples, when data are inline (included in the Command File), "line" should be read as "subcommand line," that is, everything between two subcommand delimiting slashes. It is important to have balanced parentheses in your FORTRAN statements, especially when slashes are used, thereby avoiding an erroneous interpretation as subcommand delimiter. See "Additional Options for LISREL" in Part A.

For other uses of a format statement, a FORTRAN textbook should be consulted, because there are more possibilities then can be explained here. Note, however, that LISREL allows selection (and reordering) of variables with the SE subcommand, while the SPSS system itself also offers various ways of selecting and (re)ordering variables before starting LISREL.

Rules for Record Length

The Command File normally can have records of up to 127 characters, except under IBM/MVS and IBM/CMS, where records are restricted to 80 characters.

The maximum record length for external data files depends on the mode of the input. If data are read in free format, the maximum record length is 127 characters (80 on IBM MVS and CMS). When fixed format is used, all systems support record lengths of up to 1024 characters.

Format statements are always processed like subcommand lines. Even if the format statement is given in the first line of a data file, only its first 127 (80 on MVS and CMS) columns will be processed. However, the format statement may be up to five records long.

Order of Subcommands

The order of the LISREL subcommands is arbitrary except for the following conditions (see also Table 1 below):

- After optional title subcommands, a DAta subcommand must always come first.
- The OUtput subcommand must always be last.
- LK, LE, FR, FI, EQ, PA, VA, ST, MA, PL and NF subcommands must always come after the MOdel subcommand.
- The MO subcommand is optional only if no LISREL model is analyzed. If the MO subcommand is missing, only the matrix to be analyzed will be printed out. Otherwise, the MO subcommand must appear in the Command File.
- The MATRIX subcommand is an exception to the rules above: it may be placed anywhere before the OU subcommand. But since it is the default way for data input, it need not be specified at all if there is an active file, containing the data, present.

The first (DA) and last (OU) subcommand define a subcommand set. Several subcommand sets may be stacked under the same LISREL subcommand to run several single group analyses. In the multi-group analysis (NG $>$ 1 on the first DA subcommand) the number of subcommand sets equals the NG value set. In these situations the MATRIX subcommand should come before the first OU subcommand, if used. Default input from the active file (summary data if it is a matrix system file, otherwise raw data), or input from an explicitly specified matrix system file, may not be mixed with subcommands that specify other sources for input (RA, CM, KM, MM, OM, PM, ME, SD). See also "Data Input" and "Stacked Problems, Multi-Sample Analysis, and Split Files" in Part A for further discussion of these topics, as well as the next one, multi-group or multi-sample analysis.

Command File for Multi-Sample Analysis

The subcommand sets for each group are stacked after each other[2]. They are set up as for the single group, with the following additional rules:

- NG must be defined on the DA subcommand for the first group.

[2] See Chapter 9 of *LISREL 7: A Guide to the Program and Applications.*

- For each group g ($g = 2, 3, \ldots, G$), every option or keyword that has the same value as in the previous group may be omitted.
- Pattern matrices and non-zero fixed values as well as starting values are defined as before. A matrix element such as BE(4,3), with one or two indices, refers to the element in the current group. To refer to an element in another group, use three indices, letting the first one refer to the group number. For example, BE(2,4,3) refers to β_{43} in $\mathbf{B}^{(2)}$.
- To define equality constraints between groups, specify the constrained elements as free for the first group, and equality constraints in each of the other groups. For example, if β_{43} is to be invariant over groups, specify:

  in group 1: FR BE(4,3)
  in group 2: EQ BE(1,4,3) BE(4,3)
  in group 3: EQ BE(1,4,3) BE(4,3), etc.
- If a matrix is specified as ID or ZE in group 1, it must not be specified as DI, FU or SY in subsequent groups. Similarly, if a matrix is specified as DI in group 1, it must not be specified as FU or SY in any subsequent group.
- In addition to the matrix specifications on the MO subcommand for the single group, the following specifications are possible on the MO subcommand for groups $2, 3, \ldots, G$:

  SP means that the matrix has the *same pattern* of fixed and free elements as the corresponding matrix in the previous group.

  SS means that the matrix will be given the *same starting values* as the corresponding matrix in the previous group.

  PS means *same pattern and starting values* as the corresponding matrix in the previous group.

  IN means that the matrix is *invariant* over groups, i.e., all parameter matrices have the same pattern of fixed and free elements, and all elements which are defined as free in group 1 are supposed to be equal across groups.

In principle, NY, NX, NE, and NK must be the same in all groups. However, if the numbers of variables vary over groups, it is possible to introduce pseudo-variables (observed or latent) so as to make the number of variables equal in all groups. These pseudo-variables are artificial variables that, if chosen properly, have no effects on anything.

Subcommand Overview

The remainder of this Part D presents the subcommands for LISREL problems. The subcommands are listed in alphabetical order. Table D–1 presents an overview of the LISREL subcommands in their typical order of use. The Syntax Chart that comes at the end of Part D also uses the typical order of use.

Table D–1
Overview of LISREL Subcommands

Section	Sub-command		Purpose	Position
Title(s)	/...		Problem description	Before /DA
Data input	/DA		Data specification	First subcommand
	/LA		Labels for x- and y-variables	After /DA
	/RA		Raw data input	After /DA
	/CM		Covariance matrix input	After /DA
	/KM		Correlation matrix input	After /DA
	/OM		(Special) correlation matrix input	After /DA
	/PM		(Special) correlation matrix input	After /DA
	/MM		Moment matrix input	After /DA
	/ME		Means input	After /DA
	/SD		Standard deviations input	After /DA
	/AC		Asymptotic covariance matrix input	After /DA
	/AV		Asymptotic variance matrix input	After /DA
	/DM		Diagonal weight matrix input	After /DA
	/SE		Select and reorder variables	After /DA
	/MATRIX		SPSS matrix system file input	Anywhere
Model construction	/MO		Model specification	After /DA
	/LK		Labels for ξ-variables	After /MO
	/LE		Labels for η-variables	After /MO
	/FR		Free parameters	After /MO
	/FI		Fix parameters	After /MO
	/PA		Pattern matrix to free/fix parameters	After /MO
	/EQ		Set equality constraints	After /MO
	/VA		Set fixed values	After /MO
	/ST		Set starting values	After /MO
	/MA		Matrix to set values	After /MO
	/PL		Plots of fit function	After /MO
	/NF		Never free these parameters	After /MO
Output of results	/OU	(1)	Estimation procedures	Last subcommand
		(2)	Printed output	
		(3)	Saved output	
		(4)	Estimation performance control	

Notes: The DA, MO and OU subcommands are required for a LISREL problem. The presence of other subcommands depends on the DA and MO subcommands, while title subcommands are always optional. Although the order of subcommands is relatively free, a later subcommand will overrule an earlier subcommand, insofar as the same elements are referenced.
The SPSS active system file will be used, if no explicit data input subcommands are present—either MATRIX, or one of RA, CM, KM, MM, OM or PM (and possibly ME and/or SD).

Subcommands

AC Asymptotic covariance matrix

Purpose To read the asymptotic covariance matrix of the elements of the covariance or the correlation matrix to be analyzed by the WLS method.

Syntax

```
/ AC FI = file
```

Keywords FI User-specified name of file containing the asymptotic covariance matrix.

Default: None; FI is required.

Notes The AC subcommand can only be used with MA=CM, KM or PM on the DA subcommand. It is necessary for use of the WLS estimation method, the default method (i.s.o. ML) if the AC subcommand appears. If DWLS is requested on the OU subcommand, only the diagonal elements of the asymptotic covariance matrix will be used. For ULS, GLS or ML the matrix is ignored.

The number of distinct elements in the asymptotic covariance matrix is

$\frac{1}{2}k(k+1)[\frac{1}{2}k(k+1)+1]$ if MA = CM

$\frac{1}{2}k(k-1)[\frac{1}{2}k(k-1)+1]$ if MA = KM or PM,

where k is specified by the NI keyword on the DA subcommand.

The asymptotic covariance matrix can be read only from an external file. If this matrix is produced by PRELIS, no format is necessary. Otherwise, specify the format in the first line of the external file if the elements of the asymptotic covariance matrix are in fixed format. This matrix should be read in SY form only (see the CM subcommand). Note that the FO and RE options are not allowed on the AC subcommand.

Examples

```
TITLE "PASSING FILES FROM PRELIS TO LISREL USING NAMED FILES"
DATA LIST FILE='PRL_RAW $EX74' FREE
   /1 VAR1 VAR2 VAR3 VAR4
PRELIS
   /VARIABLES=VAR1 TO VAR4
   /TYPE=COVARIANCE
   /PRINT=ACOV
   /MATRIX=OUT ('LS7_74 MATRIX')
   /WRITE=ACOV 'PRL_X74A ACOV'
LISREL
   /MATRIX=IN ('LS7_74 MATRIX')
   /"EX 7.4: ANALYSIS OF COVARIANCE MATRIX WITH WLS"
   /DA NI=4 NO=200
   /AC FI='PRL_X74A ACOV'
   /MO NX=4 NK=1 LX=FR PH=ST
   /OU
```

AV Asymptotic variances

Purpose To read the asymptotic variances of the elements of the covariance or correlation matrix to be analyzed by the DWLS method.

Syntax

```
/ AV FI = file
```

Keywords FI User-specified name of file containing the asymptotic variances.
Default: None; the FI keyword is required.

Notes The AV subcommand can be used only with MA=CM,KM or PM on the DA subcommand. It is necessary for use of the DWLS estimation method, the default method (i.s.o. ML) if the AV subcommand appears. If ULS, GLS or ML is requested on the OU subcommand, the asymptotic variances are ignored, while the choice of WLS leads to an error message.

The number of elements in the asymptotic variances file is

$\frac{1}{2}k(k+1)$ if MA = CM

$\frac{1}{2}k(k-1)$ if MA = KM or PM ,

where k is specified by the NI keyword on the DA subcommand.

The asymptotic variances can be read only from an external file. If these variances are produced by PRELIS, no format is necessary. Otherwise, specify the format in the first line of the external file if the variances are in fixed format. Note that the FO and RE options are not allowed on the AV subcommand. See the AC subcommand for an example (the logic of both subcommands is the same).

CM Covariance matrix

Purpose To read covariances for the LISREL analysis inline or from an external file. Use the `MATRIX` subcommand instead when the covariances are in a matrix system file.

Syntax

```
{ / CM } [ { SY** } ] [ FI = file [FO] [RE] ]
           { FU   }

[ / (variable format statement) ]

[ / data record [ / ... ] ]
```

Keywords

FI User-specified name of file containing the covariances.
Default: Covariances are in the Command File.

Options

SY Only elements in and below the main diagonal are present; they are read across successive rows up to and including the diagonal element.
OR

FU *All* elements in the symmetric data matrix are present and are read rowwise.
Default: SY (But see Notes below)

FO If this option appears, the variable format statement describing the data records will appear as the next line.
Default: Format statement (if any) is at the head of the covariances file.

RE If this option appears, the covariances file will be rewound after the covariances are read. Only an external file may be rewound.
Default: No rewind.

Detail Lines

(Variable format statement)
If the FI keyword and the FO option do appear (or nothing at all), and the covariances are in *fixed* format, a FORTRAN format statement, enclosed in parentheses, is inserted here to describe the column assignments of the data records.

When the covariances are in *free* format (separated by spaces, commas, slashes or return characters), which is the default, no statement is needed.

Data record (covariances)
If FI is not specified, the covariances must appear at this point in the Command File.

Notes If the MA keyword in the DA subcommand indicates that the moments about zero are to be analyzed (or the augmented moment matrix), but a covariance matrix has been input by the CM subcommand, means for the observations must be read in (see ME subcommand).

If the MA keyword in the DA subcommand indicates that the product-moment correlations are to be analyzed, but a covariance matrix has been input by the CM subcommand, standard deviations for the observations must be read in (see SD subcommand).

When neither the FU nor the SY option has been specified, and the data are in fixed format, the lower half of the matrix should be entered rowwise *as one long line*. In free format, when return characters are treated as delimiters, the matrix can be entered with one row per line. See Examples below.

Examples Given the following covariance matrix,

$$\mathbf{S} = \begin{pmatrix} 1.13 & -0.87 & 1.08 \\ -0.87 & 2.17 & 1.83 \\ 1.08 & 1.83 & 3.25 \end{pmatrix},$$

using the format F5.2, the input in the three alternatives will be (note the blanks):

```
/CM FU
/(3F5.2)
/  113  -87  108
/  -87  217  183
/  108  183  325
```

```
/CM SY
/(3F5.2)
/  113
/  -87  217
/  108  183  325
```

```
/CM
/(6F5.2)
/  113  -87  217  108  183  325
```

Another possibility is to read the matrix in free format. If blanks are used as delimiters, there is no distinction between starting a new line for each row of the matrix and reading all elements as one long line. For example, the full matrix can be read by giving

```
/CM FU
/1.13 -.87 1.08
/-.87 2.17 1.83
/1.08 1.83 3.25
```

When reading only the lower half of the matrix, the option SY is redundant (for free format).

```
/CM
/1.13 -.87 2.17 1.08 1.83 3.25
```

or, equivalently,

```
/CM
/1.13
/-.87   2.17
/1.08   1.83   3.25
```

DA

Data and problem parameters

(Required subcommand)

Purpose To specify the structure of the data and the type of moment matrix to be analyzed.

Syntax

```
/ DA NI = k [ NG = { 1** } ] [ NO = { 0**             } ]
                   { n   }            { number of cases }
            [ MA = { AM   } ] [ XM = global missing value ]
                   { CM** }
                   { KM   }
                   { MM   }
                   { OM   }
                   { PM   }
```

Keywords

NI Number of input variables
Default: None; *required keyword.*
The keyword value must be specified or the program will stop. The number of variables is limited only by machine capacity.

NG Number of groups
Default: NG = 1
For multigroup problems only (see Chapter 9 of *LISREL 7: A Guide to the Program and Applications,* as well as page A–11 and D–5 of this manual).

NO Number of cases
Default: NO = 0
If raw data are to be read from an external file or from the active file, leave NO default and the program will compute the number of cases. With summary data input using a matrix system file, NO is automatically set. Otherwise, if NO is not specified, the program will stop.

MA Type of matrix to be analyzed
Default: MA = CM
Possible values for MA:

MM	for a matrix of moments about zero
AM	for an augmented moment matrix
CM	for a covariance matrix
KM	for a matrix of product moment correlations based on raw scores or normal scores
OM	for a correlation matrix of optimal scores produced by PRELIS
PM	for a matrix which includes polychoric or polyserial correlations

XM Value for missing data. If this keyword is specified, the keyword value represents all missing values in the whole data matrix. LISREL uses *listwise deletion.* Use PRELIS for *pairwise deletion* and the SPSS system for different missing value representations, as well as other raw data problems. If raw data are input from the active file, this keyword will be automatically set, representing both user-missing values and system-missing values.

Notes The MA value specifies the kind of matrix to be *analyzed,* not the kind of matrix to be *input.* The program will convert the *input* matrix to the form specified before analysis, and starts the output with this matrix. The variables may be selected or reordered (see SE subcommand below) before the matrix is analyzed. See also "PRELIS and LISREL within SPSS" in Part A for a discussion on the relation between data input and the matrix to be analyzed.

DM User-specified diagonal weight matrix

Purpose To read user-supplied weights for DWLS analysis.

Syntax

```
/ DM FI = file
```

Keywords

FI User-specified name of file containing the diagonal weights.
Default: None; FI is required.

Notes

The DM subcommand can be used only with MA=CM, KM, PM or MM on the DA subcommand. It is necessary for the DWLS estimation method, the default method (i.s.o. ML) if the DM subcommand appears. No standard errors, t-values, chi-squares, etc., can be obtained. The diagonal weights are ignored if ULS, GLS or ML is requested on the OU subcommand.

The number of elements in the diagonal weights matrix is

$$\tfrac{1}{2}k(k+1) \text{ if MA = CM or MM}$$
$$\tfrac{1}{2}k(k-1) \text{ if MA = KM or PM ,}$$

where k is specified by the NI keyword on the DA subcommand.

The weights can be read only from an external file. Specify the format in the first line of the external file if the weights are in fixed format. Note that the FO and RE options are not allowed on the DM subcommand.

See *LISREL 7: A Guide to the Program and Applications* for a definition of the weights.

EQ Equality constraints

Purpose To constrain other parameters to be equal to a specified parameter.

Syntax

```
/ EQ list of parameter matrix elements
```

Options List of parameter matrix elements

Each element should be written as a parameter matrix name (LY, LX, BE, GA, PH, PS, TE, TD, TY, TX, AL or KA), followed by row and column index of the specific element. Row and column indices may be separated by a comma and enclosed in parentheses, like LY(3,2), LX(4,1), or separated from the matrix name and each other by spaces, like LY 3 2 LX 4 1. See Notes, below.

Notes The first parameter listed is normally a free parameter. However, it is possible to use the EQ subcommand to fix parameters and set them equal to the value of the first, fixed parameter in the list. The rules for writing the list of elements are equal to those given for the FI,FR subcommands below.

In multi-group problems, when equality constraints between groups (as opposed to within groups) are chosen, specify the constrained elements as free for the first group, and equality constraints in each of the other groups. This implies the use of a third index (referring to the group), which comes first. For example, if β_{43} is to be invariant over groups, specify:

in group 1: `FR BE(4,3)`

in group 2: `EQ BE(1,4,3) BE(4,3)`

in group 3: `EQ BE(1,4,3) BE(4,3),` etc.

FI FR — Fix matrix elements / Free matrix elements

Purpose To set specified elements fixed or free in the eight LISREL parameter matrices.

Syntax

```
/ FI list of parameter matrix elements

/ FR list of parameter matrix elements
```

Options List of parameter matrix elements

Each element should be written as a parameter matrix name (LY, LX, BE, GA, PH, PS, TE ,TD, TY, TX, AL or KA), followed by row and column index of the specific element. Row and column indices may be separated by a comma and enclosed in parentheses, like LY(3,2), LX(4,1), or separated from the matrix name and each other by spaces, like LY 3 2 LX 4 1. See Notes, below.

Notes On the MO subcommand, one can specify that an entire parameter matrix is to be fixed or free, i.e., that *all* the elements of the matrix are fixed or free. The FR and FI subcommands can be used to define the fixed-free status of *single matrix elements.*

There are three important rules for FR and FI subcommands:

- If a matrix has been specified as ZE or ID on the MO subcommand, it is not stored in computer memory and none of its elements may be referred to.
- If a matrix has been specified as DI on the MO subcommand, only the diagonal elements are stored in memory and may be referred to.
- If one specifies PH=ST on the MO subcommand, one cannot refer to any elements of $\mathbf{\Phi}$ on FI or FR subcommands (see MO subcommand above).

Any number of these subcommands may appear, and later subcommands overrule earlier subcommands with the same referents.

Examples

```
/ FIX LX(1,2),LX(2,2),LX(3,1),GA(2,2)-GA(2,5)
/ FI  LX 1 2  LX 2 2  LX 3 1  GA 2 2 -GA 2 5
```

Because both commas and parentheses may be replaced with blanks, the two subcommands are equivalent. The hyphen (or minus sign), with or without blanks, may be used for a range of parameters in consecutive order. Above, the parameters γ_{22}, γ_{23}, γ_{24} and γ_{25} are declared fixed.

It is also possible to refer to elements using linear indices, that is, counting the elements of a parameter matrix rowwise, starting at position (1,1). Assuming the LX matrix has only three columns, and GA five (and both are FU,FR), the following subcommands also are equivalent to the ones above:

```
/ FI  LX(2) LX(5) LX(7) GA(7)  - GA(10)
/ FI  LX 2  LX 5  LX 7  GA 7   - GA 10
```

Consequently, when TD has been specified as diagonal and only the diagonal elements may be referred to, the following subcommands are equivalent:

```
/ FR  TD(1,1), TD(2,2), TD(3,3)
/ FREE  TD 1 - TD 3
```

Since later subcommands overrule earlier ones, the subcommand

```
/ FR PS(1) PS(2) PS(4) - PS(7)
```

could also be specified with the two subcommands

```
/ FR  PS(1,1) - PS(7,7)
/ FI  PS(3,3)
```

provided the matrix $\boldsymbol{\Psi}$ has been specified as fixed and diagonal.

KM — Correlation matrix

Purpose To read product-moment correlations for the LISREL analysis inline or from an external file. Use the **MATRIX** subcommand when the correlations are in a matrix system file.

Syntax

```
{ / KM } [ { SY** } ] [ FI = file  [FO] [RE] ]
           { FU   }

 [ / (variable format statement) ]

 [ / data record [ / ... ] ]
```

Keywords

FI User-specified name of file containing the summary statistics.
Default: Summary statistics are in the Command File.

Options

SY Only elements in and below the main diagonal are present; they are read across successive rows up to and including the diagonal element.
OR

FU *All* elements in the symmetric data matrix are present and are read rowwise.
Default: SY (But see Notes below)

FO If this option appears, the variable format statement describing the summary statistics records will appear as the next line.
Default: Format statement (if any) is at the head of the summary statistics file.

RE If this option appears, the summary statistics file will be rewound after the summary statistics are read. Only an external file may be rewound.
Default: No rewind.

Detail Lines

(Variable format statement)

If the FI keyword and the FO option do appear (or nothing at all), and the summary statistics are in *fixed* format, a FORTRAN format statement, enclosed in parentheses, is inserted here to describe the column assignments of the data records.

When the correlations are in *free* format (separated by spaces, commas, slashes or return characters), *which is the default,* no statement is needed.

Data record (correlations)

If FI is not specified, the correlations must appear at this point in the Command File.

Notes

If the MA keyword in the DA command indicates that a covariance matrix is to be analyzed but a correlation matrix has been input by the KM subcommand, standard deviations for the observations must be read in (see SD subcommand). And if the MA keyword in the DA subcommand indicates that the moments about zero are to be analyzed (or the augmented moment matrix), both the means (ME subcommand) and the standard deviations are needed.

When neither the FU nor the SY option has been specified, and the data are in fixed format, the lower half of the matrix should be entered rowwise *as one long line.* In free format, when return characters are treated as delimiters, the matrix can be entered with one row per line. See the CM subcommand for examples (both subcommands have the same logic).

LA Labels

Purpose To assign names to each observed variable. This subcommand should *not* be used when the active file or a matrix system file is used for data input (variable names are read from the file dictionary).

Syntax

```
/ LA [ FI = file  [FO] [RE] ]

[ / (character variable format statement) ]

[ / y- and x-labels [ / ... ] ]
```

Keywords

FI User-specified name of file containing the labels.
Default: Labels are in the Command File.

Options (only relevant with FI keyword)

FO If this option appears, the variable format statement describing the label records will appear as the next line.
Default: Format statement (if any) is at the head of the label file.

RE If this option appears, the label file will be rewound after the labels are read. Only an external file may be rewound.
Default: No rewind.

Detail Lines (Character variable format statement)

If the FI keyword and the FO option do appear (or nothing at all), and the labels are in *fixed* format, a FORTRAN A-format statement, enclosed in parentheses, is inserted here to describe the column assignments of the label records.

When the labels are in *free* format (separated by spaces, commas, slashes or return characters), *which is the default,* no statement is needed.

y- and x-labels (data)

If FI is not specified, the labels must appear at this point in the Command file.

Notes If no LA subcommand appears, the default labels for observed variables (VAR 1, VAR 2, ...) are used (unless data are input from the active file or a matrix system file).

The order of the labels follows the order of the input variables. The necessary order, when both x- and y-variables are present, is y-variables first; if this is not the case, the SE subcommand below should be used to reorder the variables and their labels.

LISREL stores labels as 8-character strings. In free format longer labels will be cut off at the right. In fixed format longer labels, like (A9), will be cut off at the left. Labels shorter than eight columns will be padded with spaces to the left, in both formats.

Examples The following four examples demonstrate the various possibilities for the LA subcommand. Assume that the number of input variables equals eight, i.e., NI=8.

```
1. /LA
   /LABEL_1,,LABEL_3 LABEL_4
   /LABEL_5,LABEL_6 /
   /MODEL ...
```

The LA subcommand, without anything, indicates that format and labels will be next. However, since the labels are in free format, they follow directly. The labels are separated by a comma, a space or a slash. The double comma (,,) tells the program that no label will be given here and the default should be used. A triple comma (,,,) would skip two labels, etc. The forward slash (/) ends the list of labels before their number equals NI on the DA subcommand, otherwise it is not needed. Again, default labels will be used.

The result of example 1 would be:

```
LABEL_1   VAR 2 LABEL_3 LABEL_4 LABEL_5 LABEL_6 VAR 7 VAR 8
```

```
2. /LA
   /(4A7)
   /LABEL_1LABEL_2LABEL_3LABEL_4
   /LABEL_5LABEL_6LABEL_7LABEL_8
```

This time, a fixed format is used, informing the program that four labels of seven characters will follow. Since NI=8, two such lines are expected. In fixed format no defaults are available, of course.

```
3. /LA FI='LABELS DAT'
```

No detail lines are expected after this LA subcommand. The labels are in the external file called `LABELS DAT`. If the labels are in fixed format, this file will start with a character variable format statement; otherwise, in free format, the labels start immediately. The RE option could be added if the same labels are to be used again in the next problem of a Command File with several (stacked) subcommand sets.

```
4. /LA FI=LABEL FO
   /(8A7)
```

The difference with the example above is that the FO option indicates that a format statement will follow in the Command File. This format shows that the labels are in fixed format, with eight labels per record.

LE — Labels for latent η variables

Purpose To assign names to the η-variables.

Syntax

```
/ LE [ FI = file  [FO] [RE] ]

[ / (character variable format statement) ]

[ / eta labels [ / ... ] ]
```

Keywords

FI User-specified name of file containing the labels.
Default: Labels are in the Command File.

Options (only relevant with FI keyword)

FO If this option appears, the variable format statement describing the label records will appear as the next line.
Default: Format statement (if any) is at the head of the label file.

RE If this option appears, the label file will be rewound after the labels are read. Only an external file may be rewound.
Default: No rewind.

Detail Lines

(Character variable format statement)

If the FI keyword and the FO options do appear (or nothing at all), and the labels are in *fixed* format, a FORTRAN A-format statement, enclosed in parentheses, may be inserted here to describe the column assignments of the label records.

When the labels are in *free* format (separated by spaces, commas, slashes or return characters), *which is the default,* no statement is needed.

Data record (η-labels)

If FI is not specified, the labels must appear at this point in the Command File.

Notes If no LE subcommand appears, the default labels for latent η-variables (ETA 1, ETA 2, ...) are used.

Labels may be up to eight characters long. The syntax rules are equivalent to those for the LA subcommand.

LK Labels for latent ξ variables

Purpose To assign names to the ξ-variables.

Syntax

```
/ LK [ FI = file  [FO] [RE] ]

[ / (character variable format statement) ]

[ / ksi labels [ / ... ] ]
```

Keywords

FI User-specified name of file containing the labels.
Default: Labels are in the Command File.

Options

(only relevant with FI keyword)

FO If this option appears, the variable format statement describing the label records will appear as the next line.
Default: Format statement (if any) is at the head of the label file.

RE If this option appears, the label file will be rewound after the labels are read. Only an external file may be rewound.
Default: No rewind.

Detail Lines

(Character variable format statement)

If the FI keyword and the FO options do appear (or nothing at all), and the labels are in *fixed* format, a FORTRAN A-format statement, enclosed in parentheses, may be inserted here to describe the column assignments of the label records.

When the labels are in *free* format (separated by spaces, commas, slashes or return characters), *which is the default,* no statement is needed.

Data record (ξ-labels)

If FI is not specified, the labels must appear at this point in the Command File.

Notes

If no LK subcommand appears, the default labels for latent ξ-variables (KSI 1, KSI 2, ...) are used.

Labels may be up to eight characters long. The syntax rules are equivalent to those for the LA subcommand.

MA Matrix values

Purpose To set all elements of a parameter matrix to values specified by an input matrix; these values will be starting values for the free parameters and fixed values for the fixed parameters.

Syntax

```
/ MA  matrix name   [ FI = file  [FO] [RE] ]

 [ / (variable format statement) ]

 [ / record of matrix values [ / ... ] ]
```

Keywords

FI User-specified name of file containing the matrix values.
Default: Matrix values are in the Command File.

Options

Matrix name
Replace with the name of the parameter matrix whose elements are to be set to the fixed and/or starting values specified (LY, LX, BE, GA, PH, PS, TE, TD, TY, TX, AL or KA).

FO If this option appears, the variable format statement describing the matrix value records will appear as the next line.
Default: Format statement (if any) is at the head of the matrix values file.

RE If this option appears, the matrix values file will be rewound after the matrix values are read. Only an external file may be rewound.
Default: No rewind.

Detail Lines

(Variable format statement)
If the FI keyword and the FO option do appear (or nothing at all), and the matrix values are in *fixed* format, a FORTRAN format statement, enclosed in parentheses, may be inserted here to describe the column assignments of the matrix values.

When the matrix values are in *free* format (separated by spaces, commas, slashes or return characters), *which is the default,* no statement is needed.

Record of matrix values
If FI is not specified, the matrix values must appear at this point in the Command File.

Examples Suppose that **B** is subdiagonal, $\mathbf{\Psi}$ is symmetric and $\mathbf{\Theta}_\epsilon$ is diagonal, with the following starting values for the free parameters.

$$\mathbf{B} = \begin{pmatrix} 0 & 0 & 0 \\ 0.5 & 0 & 0 \\ 0.5 & 0.5 & 0 \end{pmatrix} \qquad \mathbf{\Psi} = \begin{pmatrix} 1.5 & & \\ 0.5 & 1.9 & \\ 0.7 & 0.5 & 1.5 \end{pmatrix}$$

$$\mathbf{\Theta}_\epsilon = \text{diag}(1.5, 1.5, 1.5)$$

These matrices could be read as:

```
/ MA BE
/(3F1.1)
/000
/500
/550
```

```
/ MA PS
/ 1.5 0.5 1.9 0.7 0.5 1.5
/ MA TE
/ 1.5 1.5 1.5
```

or, of course, from an external file (using FI = file and possibly FO and RE on the MA subcommand). With free format it is possible to read only a leading subset of elements in a matrix by terminating the list with a forward slash (/). The remaining elements will then default to zero.

See also the OU(4) subcommand below for a possible use of the MA subcommand.

MATRIX — SPSS matrix system file

Purpose To input the matrix with the summary data.

Syntax

```
/ MATRIX = { IN   ( { *  } ) **  }
                    {file}
           { NONE                }
```

Notes The IN specification designates the file containing the summary data matrix. An asterisk (*) in place of a file specification indicates that the matrix is to be read from the active file, which is also the default. Recognized Rowtypes for the summary data matrix are: CORR, COV, MOMNT, MEAN, and N. Labels for observed variables will be generated from the dictionary of the matrix file, overriding the LA subcommand, if present.

The presence of the keyword IN or NONE immediately following the subcommand name MATRIX distinguishes the SPSS LISREL MATRIX subcommand from the LISREL MA(trix) subcommand (see above).

In the event that no MATRIX subcommand, or other subcommands that input numeric data, are present, SPSS LISREL will examine the active file. If the active file is a matrix file, SPSS LISREL will determine its contents based on ROWTYPE and pass that information on to the LISREL program. If the active file is not a matrix, all numeric variables will be used and the corresponding RA and LA subcommands will be generated. The NO keyword on the DA subcommand will be set as well.

If both a MATRIX subcommand and other subcommands that input numeric data (RA, CM, KM, OM, PM, MM, SD, ME) are present, SPSS LISREL will terminate with a fatal error.

This subcommand needs exact specifications. The SPSS LISREL interface checks the subcommand set first for its presence, using the criteria mentioned above. If it is successful, it executes it. So, if this subcommand does not give expected results: (1) check your syntax (all necessary elements present and spelled correctly), and (2) check for the presence of the SPSS matrix system file (or active file).

This subcommand and its keyword **NONE** have *three* significant characters, which makes the shortest syntax: **/MAT=NON**.

See the discussions "Input Data" and "Stacked Problems and Split Files" in Part A for further details.

ME Means

Purpose To read the means of the observations inline or from an external file. Use the MATRIX subcommand if your means are in a matrix system file.

Syntax

```
/ ME [ FI = file  [FO] [RE] ]

  [ / (variable format statement) ]

  [ / data record [ / ... ] ]
```

Keywords

FI User-specified name of file containing the means.
Default: Means are in the Command File.

Options (only relevant with FI keyword)

FO If this option appears, the variable format statement describing the data records will appear as the next line.
Default: Format statement (if any) is at the head of the file with the means.

RE If this option appears, the means file will be rewound after the means are read. Only an external file may be rewound.
Default: No rewind.

Detail Lines

(Variable format statement)
If the FI keyword and the FO option do appear (or nothing at all), and the means are in *fixed* format, a FORTRAN format statement, enclosed in parentheses, is inserted here to describe the column assignments of the data records.

When the means are in *free* format (separated by spaces, commas, slashes or return characters), *which is the default,* no statement is needed.

Data record (vector of NI means)
If FI is not specified, the means must appear at this point in the Command File.

Notes The ME subcommand is used to read the standard deviations inline or from an external file. They are needed when moments about zero (or the augmented moment matrix) will be analyzed and covariances have been input, or vice versa, or when a matrix of moments about zero will be analyzed and product-moment correlations have been input (in that case, the standard deviations are also needed).

If summary data are read from the active file or a matrix system file, this subcommand may not be used. See the discussion "Input Data" in Part A for the use of means with a matrix system file.

Examples The following part of a Command File instructs the program to read first a covariance matrix; next it reads the means of the input variables from the same external file in a format specified after the ME subcommand in the Command File.

```
/DA NI=3 MA=MM
/CM FI=file
/ME FI=file FO
/(3F5.3)
```

The external file looks like:

```
(3F5.2)
  113
  -87  217
  108  183  325
 1015 2185 3753
```

The first line is the format statement for the covariance matrix, which itself occupies the next three lines, followed by the three means.

MM Moment matrix

Purpose To read moments about zero for the LISREL analysis inline or from an external file. Use the MATRIX subcommand if your moments are in a matrix system file.

Syntax

```
{ / MM } [ { SY** } ] [ FI = file  [FO] [RE] ]
           { FU   }

  [ / (variable format statement) ]

  [ / data record [ / ... ] ]
```

Keywords

FI User-specified name of file containing the moments.
Default: Moments are in the Command File.

Options

SY Only elements in and below the main diagonal are present; they are read across successive rows up to and including the diagonal element.
OR

FU *All* elements in the symmetric data matrix are present and are read rowwise.
Default: SY (But see Notes below)

FO If this option appears, the variable format statement describing the data records will appear as the next line.
Default: Format statement (if any) is at the head of the moments file.

RE If this option appears, the moments file will be rewound after the data records are read. Only an external file may be rewound.
Default: No rewind.

Detail Lines

(Variable format statement)

If the FI keyword and the FO option do appear (or nothing at all), and the data records are in *fixed* format, a FORTRAN format statement, enclosed in parentheses, is inserted here to describe the column assignments of the data records.

When the moments are in *free* format (separated by spaces, commas, slashes or return characters), *which is the default,* no statement is needed.

Data record (moments about zero)

If FI is not specified, the moments must appear at this point in the Command File.

Notes

If the MA keyword in the DA command indicates that a covariance matrix (CM) or an augmented moment matrix (AM) is to be analyzed, but a moments about zero matrix has been input by the MM subcommand, means for the observations must be read in (see ME subcommand).

When neither the FU nor the SY option has been specified, and the data are in fixed format, the lower half of the matrix should be entered rowwise *as one long line.* In free format, when return characters are treated as delimiters, the matrix can be entered with one row per line. See the CM subcommand for examples (the logic of these subcommands are similar).

MO

Model parameters

(Required subcommand)

Purpose To specify the model for the LISREL analysis.

Syntax

```
/ MO [ NY = { 0** } ] [ NX = { 0** } ]
            { p   }           { q   }

     [ NE = { 0** } ] [ NK = { 0** } ] [ FI ]
            { m   }           { n   }

     [ LY = { ID   },{ FI** } ] [ LX = { ID   },{ FI** } ]
            { IZ   } { FR   }          { IZ   } { FR   }
            { ZI   } { SP   }          { ZI   } { SP   }
            { DI   } { SS   }          { DI   } { SS   }
            { FU** } { PS   }          { FU** } { PS   }
                     { IN   }                   { IN   }

     [ BE = { ZE** },{ FI** } ] [ GA = { ID   },{ FI   } ]
            { SD   } { FR   }          { IZ   } { FR** }
            { FU   } { SP   }          { ZI   } { SP   }
                     { SS   }          { DI   } { SS   }
                     { PS   }          { FU** } { PS   }
                     { IN   }                   { IN   }

     [ PH = { ID   },{ FI   } ] [ PS = { ZE   },{ FI   } ]
            { DI   } { FR** }          { DI   } { FR** }
            { SY** } { SP   }          { SY** } { SP   }
            { ST   } { SS   }                   { SS   }
                     { PS   }                   { PS   }
                     { IN   }                   { IN   }

     [ TE = { ZE   },{ FI   } ] [ TD = { ZE   },{ FI   } ]
            { DI** } { FR** }          { DI** } { FR** }
            { SY   } { SP   }          { SY   } { SP   }
                     { SS   }                   { SS   }
                     { PS   }                   { PS   }
                     { IN   }                   { IN   }

     [ TY = { FI** } ]          [ TX = { FI** } ]
            { FR   }                   { FR   }
            { SP   }                   { SP   }
            { SS   }                   { SS   }
            { PS   }                   { PS   }
            { IN   }                   { IN   }

     [ AL = { FI** } ]          [ KA = { FI** } ]
            { FR   }                   { FR   }
            { SP   }                   { SP   }
            { SS   }                   { SS   }
            { PS   }                   { PS   }
            { IN   }                   { IN   }
```

Keywords

NY The number of y-variables in the model
Default: NY = 0

NX The number of x-variables in the model
Default: NX = 0

NE The number of η-variables in the model
Default: NE = 0

NK The number of ξ-variables in the model
Default: NK = 0

All other keywords are explained in the Notes, below.

Options

FI One option may be given on the MO subcommand, namely the logical option FIxed-x. This signifies that the x-variables are fixed or unconstrained random variables. If FI is given on the MO subcommand, the program *automatically* sets NK=NX, $\mathbf{\Lambda}_x = \mathbf{I}$, $\mathbf{\Theta}_\delta = \mathbf{0}$, $\mathbf{\Phi} = \mathbf{S}_{xx}$ (fixed), i.e., $\boldsymbol{\xi} \equiv \mathbf{x}$. The FI specification is automatically included if both NE and NK are default on the MO subcommand, i.e., for Submodel 2 the program *automatically* takes $\mathbf{x}$ to be a set of unconstrained variables (see *LISREL 7: A Guide to the Program and Applications*).

Notes

The remaining keywords specify the form and/or mode of each of the eight parameter matrices that may be used in single group analysis. The order of mode and form is immaterial; if both are used, a comma should separate them (a space is not allowed). The possible forms and modes of the matrices are summarized in Table 2. Note that ST can only be the form of the PH matrix, while SD is only possible for BE.

Table 2

Keyword Summary for Specifying the Form and Mode of the LISREL Parameter Matrices

Mathematical Notation:		$\mathbf{\Lambda}_y$	$\mathbf{\Lambda}_x$	$\mathbf{B}$	$\mathbf{\Gamma}$	$\mathbf{\Phi}$	$\mathbf{\Psi}$	$\mathbf{\Theta}_\epsilon$	$\mathbf{\Theta}_\delta$
LISREL Name:		LY	LX	BE	GA	PH	PS	TE	TD
Matrix Form:									
Zero ($\mathbf{0}$)	ZE			*			+	+	+
Identity ($\mathbf{I}$)	ID	+	+		+	+			
Identity, Zero ($\mathbf{I}\ \mathbf{0}$)	IZ	+	+		+				
Zero, Identity ($\mathbf{0}\ \mathbf{I}$)	ZI	+	+		+				
Diagonal	DI	+	+		+	+	+	*	*
Symmetric	SY					*	*	+	+
Subdiagonal	SD			+					
Standardized Symmetric	ST					+			
Full (nonsymmetric)	FU	*	*	+	*				
Matrix mode:									
Fixed	FI	*	*	*	+	+	+	+	+
Free	FR	+	+	+	*	*	*	*	*
Legend:		* Default							+ Permissible

The specification PH=ST on the MO subcommand has a special meaning.

It means that the diagonal elements of $\mathbf{\Phi}$ are fixed at unity and the off-diagonal elements are free. This specification cannot be overridden by fixing and/or freeing elements of $\mathbf{\Phi}$ on FI, FR or PA subcommands (see FI, FR subcommands above). The specifications PH=ST,FI and PH=ST,FR are not permitted.

To obtain something different from PH=ST, specify PH=FI or let PH default on the MO subcommand and then specify the fixed-free status of each element of $\mathbf{\Phi}$ on the FI or FR subcommands. For example, suppose $\mathbf{\Phi}$ is required to be

$$\mathbf{\Phi} = \begin{pmatrix} 1 & & & \\ * & 1 & & \\ 0 & 0 & * & \\ 0 & 0 & 0 & * \end{pmatrix},$$

where $*$'s are free parameters and 0's and 1's are fixed parameters. This form can be specified by:

```
/ MO ... PH=FI ...
/ FR PH(2,1) PH(3,3) PH(4,4)
/ VA 1 PH(1,1) PH(2,2)
```

In this case it is absolutely essential that a scale has been defined for ξ_3 and ξ_4 by fixing a non-zero value in columns 3 and 4 of $\mathbf{\Lambda}_x$.

The default mode for **B**, viz. FI, does not apply to the matrix form SD. The form SD sets the elements below the main diagonal free, keeping those in and above the main diagonal fixed at zero. The specification BE=SD,FI would fix the elements below the diagonal as well, and would give the same result as BE=FU (with the default mode FI).

In *multi-group problems* (NG $>$ 1), four other modes are possible that apply to the parameter matrices for the second, third, etc., group.

1. SP means that the matrix has the *same pattern* of fixed and free elements as the corresponding matrix in the previous group.

2. SS means that the matrix will be given the *same starting values* as the corresponding matrix in the previous group.

3. PS means *same pattern and starting values* as the corresponding matrix in the previous group.

4. IN means that the matrix is *invariant* over groups, *i.e.*, all parameter matrices have the same pattern of fixed and free elements, and all elements which are defined as free in the first group are supposed to be equal across groups.

See Chapter 9 of *LISREL 7: A Guide to the Program and Applications* for further information and examples.

Important Note: *The number of variables and the form (ZE, ID, DI, SY, FU) of each parameter matrix is specified on the MO line for the first group. These specifications must not be contradicted by a different specification on the MO line for subsequent groups.* This does not refer to the specification of the matrix mode (FI, FR, PS, SP, SS, or IN).

LISREL 7 now also allows for analysis of mean structures. Therefore, four new parameter matrices (vectors, actually) were added in addition to the existing eight. Table 3 lists them. See Chapter 10 of *LISREL 7: A Guide to the Program and Applications* for a complete explanation.

Table 3

Additional Parameter Matrices in LISREL

Name	Math Symbol	Order	LISREL Name	Possible Modes†
TAU-Y	τ_y	NY × 1	TY	FI,FR,IN,PS,SP,SS
TAU-X	τ_x	NX × 1	TX	FI,FR,IN,PS,SP,SS
ALPHA	α	NE × 1	AL	FI,FR,IN,PS,SP,SS
KAPPA	κ	NK × 1	KA	FI,FR,IN,PS,SP,SS

† Since these are vectors, Form is not relevant; only Mode is.

NF

No modification index for these fixed parameters

Purpose To specify elements for which modification indices should not be computed.

Syntax

```
/ NF list of parameter matrix elements
```

Options List of parameter matrix elements

Each element should be written as a parameter matrix name (LY, LX, BE, GA, PH, PS, TE, TD, TY, TX, AL or KA), followed by row and column index of the specific element. Row and column indices may be separated by a comma and enclosed in parentheses, like LY(3,2), LX(4,1), or separated from the matrix name and each other by spaces, like LY 3 2 LX 4 1. A hyphen (or minus sign) may be used for a range of parameters in consecutive order. See Notes, below.

Notes If the option MI (modification indices) is chosen on the OU subcommand and no NF subcommands appear in the Command File, the program will compute a modification index for each fixed or constrained element. Many of these may not be of interest because it is meaningless to have these elements as parameters of the model. Excluding those elements also results in faster program execution. The NF subcommand provides the possibility to specify such elements.

For example, if LX is specified as ID or IZ, modification indices for elements of $\mathbf{\Lambda}_x$ are usually of no interest. One can specify this by

$$\text{NF} \quad \text{LX}(1) - \text{LX}(k) \ ,$$

where k is the serial index of the last element of $\mathbf{\Lambda}_x$. The rules for writing the list of elements are equal to those given for the FI,FR subcommands above.

Only fixed parameters will be affected by the NF subcommand. See also Notes for FI,FR subcommands above.

Only elements in the original model will be relaxed. For example, if $\mathbf{\Theta}_\delta$ is diagonal, no off-diagonal element will be relaxed and none should appear in the NF command line. See also notes for FI,FR subcommands above.

Modification indices and estimated changes for elements specified on NF subcommands will appear as 0.000 in the output file. In the parameter specifications such elements appear as -1.

OM Optimal scores correlation matrix

Purpose To read correlations based on optimal scores or canonical correlations for the LISREL analysis inline or from an external file. Use the **MATRIX** subcommand if your correlations are in a matrix system file (generated by PRELIS).

Syntax

```
{ / OM } [ { SY** } ] [ FI = file  [FO] [RE] ]
           { FU   }

 [ / (variable format statement) ]

 [ / data record [ / ... ] ]
```

Keywords

FI User-specified name of file containing the correlations.
Default: Correlations are in the Command File.

Options

SY Only elements in and below the main diagonal are present; they are read across successive rows up to and including the diagonal element.
OR

FU *All* elements in the symmetric data matrix are present and are read rowwise.
Default: SY (But see Notes below)

FO If this option appears, the variable format statement describing the correlations records will appear as the next line.
Default: Format statement (if any) is at the head of the correlations file.

RE If this option appears, the correlations file will be rewound after the data records are read. Only an external file may be rewound.
Default: No rewind.

Detail Lines

(Variable format statement)

If the FI keyword and the FO option do appear (or nothing at all), and the correlations are in *fixed* format, a FORTRAN format statement, enclosed in parentheses, is inserted here to describe the column assignments of the data records.

When the correlations are in *free* format (separated by spaces, commas, slashes or return characters), ***which is the default,*** no statement is needed.

Data record (correlations)

If FI is not specified, the correlations must appear at this point in the Command File.

Notes

This subcommand is needed only in the exceptional case that the available data are correlations based on optimal scores that were not created by SPSS PRELIS. Normally, all correlations are generated by SPSS PRELIS and passed to LISREL in an SPSS matrix system file. The subcommand **MATRIX** should be used to input the correlations that PRELIS generates.

When neither the FU nor the SY option has been specified, and the data are in fixed format, the lower half of the matrix should be entered rowwise *as one long line.* In free format, when return characters are treated as delimiters, the matrix can be entered with one row per line. See the **CM** subcommand for examples (these subcommands share the same logic).

OU

Output requests (1)

(Required subcommand)

Purpose To establish the estimation procedures of LISREL 7.

Syntax

```
/ OU [ ME = { IV   } ] [ RC = { 0.001** } ]
            { TS   }          { value   }
            { UL   }
            { GL   }
            { ML** }
            { WL   }
            { DW   }

     [ SL = { 1**     } ]        [ NS ] [ RO ] [ AM ] [ SO ]
            { integer }
```

Keywords

ME Method of estimation.
Default: ML
Possible values:

IV	Instrumental variables
TS	Two-stage least squares
UL	Unweighted least squares
GL	Generalized least squares
ML	Maximum likelihood
WL	Generally weighted least squares
DW	Diagonally weighted least squares

RC The ridge constant. This constant will be multiplied repeatedly by 10 until the matrix becomes positive-definite. See RO option below.
Default: RC=0.001

SL The significance level of the model modification procedure expressed as an integral percent. See AM option below.
For example, SL=5 sets the significance level for the modification indices to 0.05.
Default: SL=1

Options

NS If this option appears, the program will not compute starting values. The user must supply starting values by ST or MA subcommands.

RO Ridge option.
If this option appears, the program will analyze the matrix

$$\mathbf{S} + c(\mathrm{diag}[\mathbf{S}])$$

in place of S. This option will be invoked automatically if S is not positive-definite.

AM Automatic model modification.
If this option is present, the program will modify the model sequentially by freeing at each step the fixed or constrained parameter that has the largest modification index. It will continue the modification for as long as any index is statistically significant at the α level of the SL keyword. (Use the NF command to prevent specific parameters from being modified).

SO Scaling check off.

If this option is present, the program will *not* check whether a scale has been defined for each latent variable. The SO option is needed for very special models where scales for latent variables are defined in a different way.

Notes Although the OU subcommand is presented here in four separate parts, all chosen keywords and options should be placed on one and the same OU subcommand.

An AC subcommand in the Command File changes the default method of estimation from ML to WLS, while the presence of an AV subcommand or a DM subcommand makes DWLS the default method of estimation (see AC subcommand, AV subcommand and DM subcommand above).

All options and keywords on the OU subcommand may be omitted, but a subcommand with the two characters OU must be included as the last subcommand of the Command File.

OU Output requests (2)

Purpose To select the printed output of LISREL 7.

Syntax

```
/OU  [ SE ] [ TV ] [ PC ]

     [ RS ] [ EF ] [ MR ] [ MI ] [ FS ] [ SS ] [ SC ]

     [ ALL ] [ { TO    } ] [ND = number of decimals ]
               { WP ** }
```

Keywords and Options

SE	Standard errors
TV	*t*-values (estimate/standard error)
PC	Correlation matrix of parameter estimators
RS	Residuals, standardized residuals, Q-plot and fitted covariance (or correlation, or moment) matrix $\hat{\Sigma}$
EF	Total effects and indirect effects
MR	Miscellaneous results
MI	Model modification indices
FS	Factor-scores regression
SS	Standardized solution
SC	Solution completely standardized
ALL	**Print everything** (may be given as "AL")
TO	Print 80 characters per record (TO for Terminal Output)
WP	Print 132 characters per record (default; WP for Wide Print)
ND	Number of decimals (0–8) in the printed output **Default**: ND = 3

OU — Output requests (3)

Purpose To save various matrices in specified external files at termination.

Syntax

```
/OU [ matrix name = file [ ... ] ]
```

Keywords matrix name

Replace with the matrix name to be saved.
Possible names:
LY, LX, BE, GA, PH, PS, TE, TD, TY, TX, AL, KA
or

- MA The matrix analyzed after selection and/or reordering of variables
- SI The fitted (moment, covariance, or correlation) matrix, $\hat{\boldsymbol{\Sigma}}$ (SI for SIgma)
- RM The regression matrix of latent variables on observed variables. Printout of the matrix must also have been requested with the FS option described under output requests(2) above
- EC The estimated asymptotic covariance matrix of the LISREL parameter estimates.

Notes The matrices are written in format (6D13.6), preceded by a line with the format and the name of the saved matrix. This format means that each value occupies 13 columns, the last six being the decimal places, and that there are six values per record.

OU

Output requests (4)

Purpose To control the performance of the LISREL 7 iterative estimation procedures.

Syntax

```
/ OU  [ TM = { max seconds } ]
             { 60**        }

      [ IT = { max iterations                    } ]
             { three times all free parameters** }

      [ AD = { OFF     } ]
             { integer }
             { 10**    }

      [ EP = { 0.000001**            } ]
             { convergence criterion }
```

Keywords

TM The maximum number of CPU seconds allowed for the current problem.
Default: TM = 60

IT Maximum number of iterations allowed for the current problem.
Default: IT = three times the number of free parameters

AD Check the admissibility of the solution after m iterations and stop the program if the admissibility check fails. Note that the program will always check the admissibility of the final solution, regardless of the value of the AD keyword.
Default: AD=10
or
Turn off the admissibility check: AD=OFF.

EP Convergence criterion, epsilon. The default value normally results in a solution that is accurate to three significant digits. However, this cannot be guaranteed for all problems.
Default: EPS=0.000001

Notes If t seconds are exceeded, the iterations are stopped and the current "solution" is written onto a file called DUMP unless another file is specified on the OU subcommand (see OU(3), above). The "solution" LY, LX, BE, GA, PH, PS, TE and TD (and possibly TY, TX, AL and KA) is written in format (6D13.6), and is preceded by a line with this format and the name of the matrix. A matrix saved in this way can be read by LISREL with an MA subcommand (see above). For example:

MA LY FI=DUMP

The program will also terminate and write an intermediate solution to "DUMP," if convergence is not achieved within n iterations or if numerical instabilities are encountered.

PA Pattern matrix

Purpose To set elements of the LISREL parameter matrices Fixed or Free using a pattern of 1's and 0's ($1 \equiv$ Free; $0 \equiv$ Fixed).

Syntax

```
/ PA  matrix name  [ FI = file  [FO] [RE] ]

  [ / (integer format statement) ]

  [ / pattern record [ / ... ] ]
```

Keywords

FI User-specified name of file containing the pattern matrix.
Default: Pattern matrix is in the Command File.

Options

Matrix name
Replace with the name of the parameter matrix whose elements are to be set fixed or free (LY, LX, BE, GA, PH, PS, TE, TD, TY, TX, AL or KA).

FO If this option appears, the integer format statement describing the pattern matrix will appear as the next line.
Default: Format statement (if any) is at the head of the pattern matrix file.

RE If this option appears, the pattern matrix file will be rewound after the labels are read. Only an external file may be rewound.
Default: No rewind.

Detail Lines

(Integer format statement)
If the FI keyword and the FO option do appear (or nothing at all), and the pattern matrix is in *fixed* format, a FORTRAN I-format statement, enclosed in parentheses, may be inserted here to describe the column assignments of the pattern matrix records.

When the pattern matrix is in *free* format (separated by spaces, commas, slashes or return characters), *which is the default,* no statement is needed.

Pattern record
If FI is not specified, the pattern matrix must appear at this point in the Command File.

Notes One of these subcommand lines may appear for each matrix.

If the pattern matrix is in free format (with 1 and 0 elements separated by spaces, commas or return characters) and the number of 1's and 0's is less than the number of elements in the matrix, the pattern must end with a forward slash (/). The elements after the slash default to 0's.

Examples

1. The following are four alternative ways of reading the pattern matrix for

$$\mathbf{\Gamma} = \begin{pmatrix} free & fixed & fixed \\ fixed & free & free \end{pmatrix}$$

```
/ PA GA
/ (6I1)
/100011
```

```
/ PA GA
/(3I1)
/100
/011

/PA GA
/ 1 0 0 0 1 1

/ PA GA
/ 1 0 0
/ 0 1 1
```

2. If a matrix is symmetric, only the elements in the lower half, including the diagonal, should be read. If a matrix is specified to be diagonal, only the diagonal elements should be read. For example, if $\mathbf{\Phi}(4 \times 4)$ is symmetric with fixed diagonal elements and free off-diagonal elements, and if $\mathbf{\Psi}(4 \times 4)$ is diagonal, with elements ψ_{11} and ψ_{33} fixed and ψ_{22} and ψ_{44} free, the pattern matrices are read as:

```
/ PA PH
/ 0 1 0 1 1 0 1 1 1 0
/ PA PS
/ 0 1 0 1
```

3. Suppose the symmetric matrix $\mathbf{\Phi}$ of order 10×10 should be specified such that only the first five diagonal elements should be free, all other elements being fixed. This pattern matrix can be read as:

```
/ PA PH
/ 1
/ 0 1
/ 0 0 1
/ 0 0 0 1
/ 0 0 0 0 1/
```

The forward slash (/) at the end of the last record implies that the remaining elements will all be zero. Data containing repetitions of the same number or group of numbers can be read very conveniently. For example, the matrix $\mathbf{\Phi}$ can also be read as:

```
/ PA PH
/ 1 0 1 2*0 1 3*0 1 4*0 1/
```

Here, 3*0 is equivalent to 0 0 0. Note again the LISREL slash at the end, indicating that no more data will follow.

4. Suppose one wants to read the following pattern matrix for $\mathbf{\Lambda}_x$.

$$\begin{pmatrix} 1 & 0 & 0 \\ 1 & 0 & 0 \\ 1 & 0 & 0 \\ 0 & 1 & 0 \\ 0 & 1 & 0 \\ 0 & 1 & 0 \\ 0 & 0 & 1 \\ 0 & 0 & 1 \\ 0 & 0 & 1 \end{pmatrix}$$

This can be read as:

```
/ PA LX
/ 3*(1 0 0) 3*(0 1 0) 3*(0 0 1)
```

or even more simply (by omitting the asterisks) as:

```
/ PA LX
/ 3(1 0 0) 3(0 1 0) 3(0 0 1)
```

PL Plots

Purpose To plot the fit functions for ULS, GLS, ML, WLS or DWLS against any parameter, fixed or free.

Syntax

```
/ PL list of parameter matrix elements [ FROM a TO b ]
```

Options List of parameter matrix elements

Each element should be written as a parameter matrix name (LY, LX, BE, GA, PH, PS, TE, TD, TY, TX, AL or KA), followed by row and column index of the specific element. Row and column indices may be separated by a comma and enclosed in parentheses, like LY(3,2), LX(4,1), or separated from the matrix name and each other by spaces, like LY 3 2 LX 4 1. See Notes, below.

a, *b* The *range* of parameter values to be plotted.

Default: An approximate 95 percent confidence interval for free parameters. For fixed parameters, the predicted estimated change in the parameter when set free.

Notes The parameter plots in LISREL 6 and LISREL 7 differ. The plot in LISREL 7 is a plot of the *concentrated* fit function, i.e., for each value of $\boldsymbol{\theta}$, the *minimum* of the fit function with respect to all other free parameters is plotted.

Several PL commands may be included in each problem, but the total number of plots cannot exceed 10.

The rules for writing the list of elements are equal to those given for the FI,FR subcommands above.

Examples To plot the parameters LX(2,1), LY(4,3), TD(1,1), write:

```
/ PL LX(2,1) LY(4,3) TD(1,1)
```

And to plot TD(1,1) and TD(2,2) from 0.4 to 0.5, write:

```
/ PL TD(1,1) TD(2,2) FROM 0.4 TO 0.5
```

PM Polychoric and/or polyserial correlations

Purpose To read polychoric and/or polyserial correlations for the LISREL analysis in-line or from an external file. Use the **MATRIX** subcommand if the correlations are in a matrix system file.

Syntax

```
{ / PM } [ { SY** } ] [ FI = file  [FO] [RE] ]
           { FU   }

   [ / (variable format statement) ]

   [ / data record [ / ... ] ]
```

Keywords

FI User-specified name of file containing the correlations.
Default: Correlations are in the Command File.

Options

SY Only elements in and below the main diagonal are present; they are read across successive rows up to and including the diagonal element.
OR

FU *All* elements in the symmetric data matrix are present and are read rowwise.
Default: SY (But see Notes below)

FO If this option appears, the variable format statement describing the data records will appear as the next line.
Default: Format statement (if any) is at the head of the correlations file.

RE If this option appears, the correlations file will be rewound after the data records are read. Only an external file may be rewound.
Default: No rewind.

Detail Lines

(Variable format statement)

If the FI keyword and the FO option do appear (or nothing at all), and the correlations are in *fixed* format, a FORTRAN format statement, enclosed in parentheses, is inserted here to describe the column assignments of the data records.

When the correlations are in *free* format (separated by spaces, commas, slashes or return characters), *which is the default,* no statement is needed.

Data record (correlations)

If FI is not specified, the correlations must appear at this point in the Command File.

Notes

In general, this subcommand is needed only in the exceptional case that the available data are polychoric and/or polyserial correlations that were not created by SPSS PRELIS. In the latter case the subcommand **MATRIX** should be used to input the correlations that PRELIS generates.

When neither the FU nor the SY option has been specified, and the data are in fixed format, the lower half of the matrix should be entered rowwise *as one long line.* In free format, when return characters are treated as delimiters, the matrix can be entered with one row per line. See the **CM** subcommand for examples (these subcommands have a similar syntactical logic).

RA Raw data

Purpose To input case records containing values of the variables for analysis. Do not use this subcommand if the raw data are in the active file.

Syntax

```
/ RA [ FI = file  [FO] [RE] ]

  [ / (variable format statement) ]

  [ / data record [ / ... ] ]
```

Keywords
FI User-specified name of file containing the observations.
Default: Observations are in the Command File.

Options (only relevant with FI keyword)
FO If this option appears, the variable format statement describing the observation records will appear as the next line.
Default: Format statement (if any) is at the head of the observation file.
RE If this option appears, the observation file will be rewound after the observations are read. Only an external file may be rewound.
Default: No rewind.

Detail Lines (Variable format statement)
If the FI keyword and the FO option do appear (or nothing at all), and the observations are in *fixed* format, a FORTRAN format statement, enclosed in parentheses, is inserted here to describe the column assignments of the observation records.

When the observations are in *free* format (separated by spaces, commas, slashes or return characters), *which is the default,* no statement is needed.

Data record
If FI is not specified, the observations must appear at this point in the Command File.

Notes The RA and LA subcommands are automatically set if the raw data are in the active file. All numeric variables in the file will be used. If raw data are read inline or from an external file, and the user sets the **RA** subcommand, the following applies.

The raw data are read one case after another. There must be NI data values (see DA subcommand) for each case. Preferably, data are read from an external file. Then the program will determine the sample size if NO on the DA subcommand is default or set to 0. Or if NO is erroneously set too large, the program will terminate input when an end-of-file is encountered and will use the correct case count in the computations. If NO is set too small, only NO cases will be read, regardless of how many cases exist. When the data are included in the Command File, NO should indicate the number of cases correctly, otherwise the program will stop with an error message.

When reading a raw data case in free format, blanks, commas and return characters are used as delimiters in an external file, while blanks, commas and forward slashes are used when the data appear in the Command File. The following options are available:

- Ending a case record with a forward slash may be used to indicate that all remaining data values for this case are the same as the corresponding data values for the previous case.
- Two consecutive commas may be used to specify that the corresponding data value for the previous case should be inserted between the commas. Three consecutive commas imply that two data values from the previous case will be inserted, etc.
- Repetitions of the same data value can be specified by an * preceded by a repeat factor. For example, 4*1 means 1 1 1 1.
- LISREL interprets all data values as floating point decimal numbers However, for data values that are integers, the decimal point may be omitted.

Examples

1. Raw data are read from an external file. The data are in fixed format and the format statement follows the RA subcommand in the Command File, as indicated by the option FO. The number of observations will be computed by the program from the data, because the NO keyword on the DA subcommand was not given.

```
/ DA NI=5
/ RA FI=DATA FO
/ (5F3.1)
```

2. Raw data follow the RA subcommand in free format.

```
/ DA NI=5 NO=20
/ RA
/ 3.5 4.2 6.8, 9.3, 10.1
/ 3.7 5.1 /
/ 3.2 ,, 7.2 3.4 9
/ 2*3.8 4.1
/ 6.2 4.1

   ⋮
```

The first four cases of the raw data are equivalent to:

```
(5F3.1)
 35 42 68 93101
 37 51 68 93101
 32 51 72 34 90
 38 38 41 62 41
```

SD Standard deviations

Purpose To read the standard deviations of the observations inline or from an external file. Do not use this subcommand if summary data are input from a matrix system file.

Syntax

```
/ SD [ FI = file  [FO] [RE] ]

  [ / (variable format statement) ]

  [ / data record [ / ... ] ]
```

Keywords

FI User-specified name of file containing the standard deviations.
Default: Standard deviations are in the Command File.

Options (only relevant with FI keyword)

FO If this option appears, the variable format statement describing the standard deviation records will appear as the next line.
Default: Format statement (if any) is at the head of the file with the standard deviations.

RE If this option appears, the standard deviations file will be rewound after the standard deviations are read. Only an external file may be rewound.
Default: No rewind.

Detail Lines (Variable format statement)

If the FI keyword and the FO option do appear (or nothing at all), and the standard deviations are in *fixed* format, a FORTRAN format statement, enclosed in parentheses, is inserted here to describe the column assignments of the standard deviation records.

When the standard deviations are in *free* format (separated by spaces, commas, slashes or return characters), ***which is the default,*** no statement is needed.

Data record (vector of NI standard deviations)

If FI is not specified, the standard deviations must appear at this point in the Command File.

Notes For an example, see the `ME` subcommand thas has a similar logic as the `SD` subcommand.

The `SD` subcommand is used to input the standard deviations inline or from an external file. They are needed when a covariance matrix will be analyzed and product-moment correlations have been input, or vice versa. Or when a matrix of moments about zero will be analyzed and product-moment correlations have been input (in that case the means are also needed).

If summary data are read from the active file or a matrix system file, this subcommand may not be used. See the discussion "Input Data" in Part A for the use of standard deviations with a matrix system file.

SE — Select and reorder variables

Purpose To select in any order any number of variables from the NI input variables.

Syntax

```
/ SE [ FI = file ]

[ / variable names [ / ... ] ]
```

Keywords

FI User-specified name of file containing the list of variable names or numbers.
Default: The list of names follows the subcommand.

Detail Lines

Variable names (or numbers)
If FI is not specified, the list of variables must appear at this point in the Command File.

Notes

The selected variables should be listed either by number or by label (see: LA subcommand) in the order that they are wanted in the model and *the y-variables should be listed first.*

The variable names are listed in free-format separated by blanks, commas, slashes or return characters (a variable format statement is not required).

If the number of names in the list is less than NI, the list must terminate with a forward slash (/).

The selection and reordering of variables specified by the SE command will affect not only the covariance or correlation matrix to be analyzed but also the asymptotic covariance matrix or the asymptotic variances if these have been entered.

The selection and reordering will be executed after requested transformation of input data (for instance, correlations plus standard deviations in covariances) has taken place. Thus, all input data should conform to the number of input variables (`NI` on the `DA` subcommand) and the order before any selection and/or reordering.

ST Starting values

Purpose To assign starting values for iterative estimation of free parameters.

Syntax

```
/ ST numerical value { list of parameter matrix elements }
                     { ALL                               }
```

Options

numerical value

Numerical value to be assigned (with decimal point).

Default: none; required option.

List of parameter matrix elements

Each element should be written as a parameter matrix name (LY, LX, BE, GA, PH, PS, TE, TD, TY, TX, AL or KA), followed by row and column index of the specific element. Row and column indices may be separated by a comma and enclosed in parentheses, like LY(3,2), LX(4,1), or separated from the matrix name and each other by spaces, like LY 3 2 LX 4 1. See Notes, below.

ALL Set all *free* elements in all parameter matrices to starting value (with ST; see Notes, below). "ALL" may *not* be given as "AL."

Default: ST values will be computed by the program, if possible.

Notes Setting ST values to good approximations from similar analyses may save some computing time. Otherwise, the default values estimated by IV or TSLS will be supplied by the program.

The rules for writing the list of elements are equal to those given for the FI,FR subcommands above.

This subcommand may appear any number of times. Values in later subcommands override those in earlier subcommands with the same referents.

The VA (see below) and ST subcommands are equivalent and may be used synonymously. Whether the assigned value will be a starting value or a fixed value is dependent on the mode of each element, as specified in the relevant subcommands. There is one exception, however. When a *range* of elements is specified, as LY(1,1)–LY(2,2), then ST assigns values only to the free parameters in the range, while VA sets both free and fixed parameters. Hence, the option "ALL" behaves differently for VA and ST, and, although allowed for the VA subcommand, it is only useful for the ST subcommand.

Examples

1. Suppose that $\mathbf{B}$ is subdiagonal, $\mathbf{\Psi}$ is symmetric and $\mathbf{\Theta}_\epsilon$ is diagonal, with the following starting values for the free parameters.

$$\mathbf{B} = \begin{pmatrix} 0 & 0 & 0 \\ 0.5 & 0 & 0 \\ 0.5 & 0.5 & 0 \end{pmatrix} \qquad \mathbf{\Psi} = \begin{pmatrix} 1.5 & & \\ 0.5 & 1.9 & \\ 0.7 & 0.5 & 1.5 \end{pmatrix}$$

$$\mathbf{\Theta}_\epsilon = \mathrm{diag}(1.5, 1.5, 1.5)$$

The starting values for the free parameters may then be set by the following ST subcommands.

```
/ ST  0.5 BE(2,1) BE(3,1)-BE(3,2) PS(2,1) PS(3,2)
/ ST  1.5 PS(1,1) PS(3,3) TE(1)-TE(3)
/ ST  1.9 PS(2,2)
/ ST  0.7 PS(3,1)
```

Whenever a range of elements is specified, only those elements in this range which have been specified as non-fixed (free or constrained) elements will be set. Thus, the first of the ST subcommands above can also be written, with the same effect, as:

```
/ ST 0.5 BE(1,1)-BE(3,3) PS(2,1) PS(3,2)
```

2. All non-fixed elements in all parameter matrices are set at the same starting value. Next, PS(1,1) is assigned a different starting value.

```
/ ST 0.5 ALL
/ ST 5 PS 1 1
```

Note that the option "ALL" must be entered with all *three* significant characters.

Title

Title lines are optional. The LISREL subcommands for each problem may be preceded by one or more title records naming and describing the problem. The program will read, and print at the head of the problem output, all lines preceding the DA (Data description) subcommand; thereafter it prints only the first title line as a heading for each section of output. The title records must *not* use the characters `DA`, `Da`, `dA`, or `da` as the first two non-blank characters. When one or more apostrophes (single quote) appear in a title line, use double quotes to protect them. Blank title lines, for vertical spacing, should also be enclosed in double (or single) quotes, otherwise one of the slashes will be interpreted as a LISREL end-of-data slash (see "Syntax Development" in Part A). In general, it is recommended to enclose all title lines in double quotes.

Note that LISREL also allows blank lines at other places in the Command File, but *not* before detail lines like format statements or data. Such blank lines should also be protected by double (or single) quotes.

Examples

```
/"Modified Model for Performance and Satisfaction              "
/"References                                                   "
/"Bagozzi, R.P.                                                "
/" 'Performance and satisfaction in an industrial sales force"
/"  An examination of their antecedents and simultaneity.'     "
/"     Journal of marketing, 1980, 44, 65-77.                  "
/"                                                             "
/"Joreskog, K.G. and Sorbom, D.                                "
/" 'Recent developments in structural equation modeling.'      "
/"     Journal of marketing research, 1982, 19, 404-416        "
/"                                                             "
/DATA   NI=8 NO=122
/' '
/MODEL  NY=3 NX=5 ...
```

VA Fixed values

Purpose To assign numerical values to fixed parameters.

Syntax

```
/ VA numerical value { list of parameter matrix elements }
                     { ALL                               }
```

Options

numerical value

Numerical value to be assigned (with decimal point).

Default: none; required option.

List of parameter matrix elements

Each element should be written as a parameter matrix name (LY, LX, BE, GA, PH, PS, TE, TD, TY, TX, AL or KA), followed by row and column index of the specific element. Row and column indices may be separated by a comma and enclosed in parentheses, like LY(3,2), LX(4,1), or separated from the matrix name and each other by spaces, like LY 3 2 LX 4 1. See Notes, below.

ALL (See Notes, below.) "ALL" may *not* be given as "AL."

Default: VA values are zero. ST values will be computed by the program, if possible.

Notes Setting elements fixed by the FI, PA or EQ commands does not set their values. All elements, whether fixed, free or constrained, are zero by default.

The rules for writing the list of elements are equal to those given for the FI,FR subcommands above.

This subcommand may appear any number of times. Values in later subcommands override those in earlier commands with the same referents.

The VA and ST subcommands are equivalent and may be used synonymously. Whether the assigned value will be a starting value or a fixed value is dependent on the mode of each element, as specified in the relevant subcommands. There is one exception, however. When a range of elements is specified, as LY(1,1)–LY(2,2), then fixed elements in this range are changed by VA, but not by ST. Hence, the option "ALL" behaves differently for VA and ST, and, although allowed for the VA subcommand, it is useful only for the ST subcommand.

Examples

```
/ VA 1.5 LX(2,1) LY(6,2) GA(1,2)
```

assigns the value 1.5 to $\lambda_{21}^{(x)}$, $\lambda_{62}^{(y)}$, and γ_{12}.

LISREL Syntax

Syntax Chart LISREL

```
Title line(s)   [ / "title line" [ / ... ] ]

Data input      / DA NI = k [ NG = { 1** } ]  [ NO = { 0**              } ]
                                   { n   }          { number of cases }

                       [ MA = { AM   } ] [ XM = global missing value ]
                              { CM** }
                              { KM   }
                              { MM   }
                              { OM   }
                              { PM   }

                [ / LA [ FI = file  [FO] [RE] ] ]

                      [ / (character variable format statement) ]

                      [ / y- and x-labels [ / ... ] ]

                [ / MATRIX = { IN ( { *    } )** } ]
                                    { file }
                             { NONE              }

                [ / RA [ FI = file  [FO] [RE] ] ]

                      [ / (variable format statement) ]

                      [ / data record [ / ... ] ]

                [ { / CM } [ { SY** } ] [ FI = file  [FO] [RE] ] ]
                  { / KM }   { FU   }
                  { / OM }
                  { / PM }
                  { / MM }

                      [ / (variable format statement) ]

                      [ / data record [ / ... ] ]

                [ / ME [ FI = file  [FO] [RE] ] ]

                      [ / (variable format statement) ]

                      [ / data record [ / ... ] ]
```

```
[ / SD [ FI = file  [FO] [RE] ] ]

      [ / (variable format statement) ]

      [ / data record [ / ... ] ]

[ / AC FI = file ]

[ / AV FI = file ]

[ / DM FI = file ]

[ / SE [ FI = file ] ]

      [ / variable names [ / ... ] ]
```

Model construction

```
/ MO [ NY = { 0** } ] [ NX = { 0** } ]
            { p   }            { q   }

      [ NE = { 0** } ] [ NK = { 0** } ] [ FI ]
             { m   }          { n   }

      [ LY = { ID   },{ FI** } ] [ LX = { ID   },{ FI** } ]
             { IZ   } { FR   }          { IZ   } { FR   }
             { ZI   } { SP   }          { ZI   } { SP   }
             { DI   } { SS   }          { DI   } { SS   }
             { FU** } { PS   }          { FU** } { PS   }
                      { IN   }                   { IN   }

      [ BE = { ZE** },{ FI** } ] [ GA = { ID   },{ FI   } ]
             { SD   } { FR   }          { IZ   } { FR** }
             { FU   } { SP   }          { ZI   } { SP   }
                      { SS   }          { DI   } { SS   }
                      { PS   }          { FU** } { PS   }
                      { IN   }                   { IN   }

      [ PH = { ID   },{ FI   } ] [ PS = { ZE   },{ FI   } ]
             { DI   } { FR** }          { DI   } { FR** }
             { SY** } { SP   }          { SY** } { SP   }
             { ST   } { SS   }                   { SS   }
                      { PS   }                   { PS   }
                      { IN   }                   { IN   }

      [ TE = { ZE   },{ FI   } ] [ TD = { ZE   },{ FI   } ]
             { DI** } { FR** }          { DI** } { FR** }
             { SY   } { SP   }          { SY   } { SP   }
                      { SS   }                   { SS   }
                      { PS   }                   { PS   }
                      { IN   }                   { IN   }

      [ TY = { FI** } ]          [ TX = { FI** } ]
             { FR   }                   { FR   }
             { SP   }                   { SP   }
             { SS   }                   { SS   }
             { PS   }                   { PS   }
             { IN   }                   { IN   }
```

```
[ AL = { FI** } ]          [ KA = { FI** } ]
       { FR   }                   { FR   }
       { SP   }                   { SP   }
       { SS   }                   { SS   }
       { PS   }                   { PS   }
       { IN   }                   { IN   }

[ / LK [ FI = file  [FO] [RE] ] ]

      [ / (character variable format statement) ]

      [ / ksi labels [ / ... ] ]

[ / LE [ FI = file  [FO] [RE] ] ]

      [ / (character variable format statement) ]

      [ / eta labels [ / ... ] ]

[ / FR list of parameter matrix elements ]

[ / FI list of parameter matrix elements ]

[ / PA  matrix name  [ FI = file  [FO] [RE] ]  ]

      [ / (integer format statement) ]

      [ / pattern record [ / ... ] ]

[ / EQ list of parameter matrix elements ]

[ / VA numerical value { list of parameter matrix elements } ]
                       { ALL                              }

[ / ST numerical value { list of parameter matrix elements } ]
                       { ALL                              }

[ / MA  matrix name  [ FI = file  [FO] [RE] ]  ]

      [ / (variable format statement) ]

      [ / record of matrix values [ / ... ] ]

[ / PL list of parameter matrix elements [ FROM a TO b ] ]

[ / NF list of parameter matrix elements ]
```

Output of results
(1) Estimation procedures

```
/ OU [ ME = { IV   } ] [ RC = { 0.001** } ] [ SL = { 1**     } ]
            { TS   }          { value   }          { integer }
            { UL   }
            { GL   }
            { ML** }
            { WL   }
            { DW   }

     [ NS ] [ RO ] [ AM ] [ SO ]
```

(2) Printed output

```
[ SE ] [ TV ] [ PC ]

[ RS ] [ EF ] [ MR ] [ MI ] [ FS ] [ SS ] [ SC ]

[ ALL ] [ { TO   } ] [ND = number of decimals ]
          { WP** }
```

(3) Saved output

```
[ matrix name = { file        } [ ... ] ]
```

(4) Estimation performance control

```
[ TM = { maximum seconds } ]
       { 60**            }

[ IT = { maximum iterations                } ]
       { three times all free parameters** }

[ AD = { OFF     } ] [ EP = { 0.000001**            } ]
       { integer }          { convergence criterion }
     { 10**    }
```

Syntax Notation

- Subcommand order is important (see Table D–1 on page D–7).
- Equals signs are required.
- Uppercase elements are subcommands, keywords or options. They must be entered as they appear, or they may be lengthened (LABELS instead of LA, for instance). The added SPSS MATRIX subcommand and its keyword NONE may be truncated to the first *three* characters. Thus, everything else, except for the ALL option on the VA and ST subcommand, has *two* significant characters.
- Lowercase elements describe items to be filled in by the user.
- Special delimiters should be entered exactly as shown.
- Slashes are required between subcommands. A slash is also required immediately following the command name, i.e., before the first subcommand. A slash following the last subcommand is optional.
- Use blanks to separate subcommand names, keywords, and options.
- Square brackets `[]` enclose optional specifications not necessary for the correct completion of the command. The brackets should not be coded.
- Braces {} enclose alternative specifications. One (and only one) of these specifications must be entered in order to complete the specifications correctly. The braces themselves should not be coded.
- Ellipses `...` indicate the possibility of repeating an element or an entire sequence of elements.
- **`Boldface`** and starred (`**`) entries denote default specifications.
- For format statements, see page D–3.
- Each element in the `list of parameter matrix elements` should be written as a parameter matrix name (LY, LX, BE, GA, PH, PS, TE, TD, TY, TX, AL, or KA), followed by row and column index (or linear index) of the specific element. Row and column indices may be separated by a comma and enclosed in parentheses, like LY(3,2),LX(4,1), or separated from the matrix name and each other by spaces, like LY 3 2 LX 4 1.
- The order of the form and mode values for the parameter matrices on the MO subcommand is optional, but if both are given, a comma in between is required.

Examples

- *PRELIS Examples*
- *A LISREL Example*

Contents

PRELIS Examples

SPSS PRELIS can be used in many ways considering all the ways variables can be declared and transformed and all the different types of moment matrices that can be obtained. Only a very small fraction of these can be shown here. The ones we have chosen illustrate the more important features that PRELIS offers.

The subcommands that produced the examples are typeset somewhat larger than the output. Sections of the output (slightly edited) are presented, together with explanations and comments.

Compute Matrix of Polyserial and Polychoric Correlations

Data for Example 1A consist of the first hundred cases of the artificial data described in Chapter 1 of Part B. We examine the data and use the TYPE=POLYCHOR subcommand to compute the matrix of polychoric and polyserial correlations.

There are six variables. Two of them (variables 1 and 5) are continuous, labeled CONTIN1 and CONTIN2. Four others (variables 2, 3, 4, and 6) are ordinal, labeled ORDINAL1, ORDINAL2, ORDINAL3, and ORDINAL4.

The number "−9" is used to represent missing values.

```
TITLE "PRELIS test on artificial data; 1A"
DATA LIST FILE=file FREE
 /1 CONTIN1 ORDINAL1 ORDINAL2 ORDINAL3
    CONTIN2 ORDINAL4
MISSING VALUES CONTIN1 TO ORDINAL4 (-9)
PRELIS
   /VARIABLES = CONTIN1 (CO) ORDINAL1 TO ORDINAL3 (OR)
                CONTIN2 (CO) ORDINAL4 (OR)
   /MISSING   = PAIRWISE EXCLUDE
   /TYPE      = POLY
   /MATRIX    = NONE
   /PRINT     = NONE
FINISH
```

The line width to be used for output (screen or printer) could be changed with the SPSS SET WIDTH command by specifying a value of 132, the only alternative to the default of 80 columns wide. The MATRIX and PRINT subcommands may be omitted here, since both have NONE as defaults. The specification POLY instead of POLYCHOR is sufficient; in fact, POL would have been enough, because only the first three characters are relevant. The minimum PRELIS specifications for this example are:

```
PRELIS CONTIN1 (CO) ORDINAL1 TO ORDINAL3 (OR)
       CONTIN2 (CO) ORDINAL4 (OR) /MIS PAI /TYP POL
```

Note, however, that the list of variables should immediately follow the PRELIS command if the optional VAR subcommand name is omitted.

```
                    P R E L I S  1.12
                           BY
            KARL G JORESKOG AND DAG SORBOM

THE FOLLOWING PRELIS CONTROL LINES HAVE BEEN READ :
DA NI=6 NO=0 MI=-0.989898D+37 MC=15 TR=PA
RAW-DATA-FROM FILE = DATA.100
LA
CONTIN1 ORDINAL1 ORDINAL2 ORDINAL3 CONTIN2 ORDINAL4
RA FI=PRLDD22
OR ORDINAL1
OR ORDINAL2
OR ORDINAL3
CO CONTIN2
OR ORDINAL4
OU MA=PM SM=PRLDD23
```

The PRELIS output starts with the translated SPSS subcommands. Unless the user happens to know the original PRELIS stand-alone version, this is not of much information. The SPSS user will check the PRELIS subcommands as they are written on the log to verify correct input.

```
DISTRIBUTION OF MISSING VALUES
TOTAL SAMPLE SIZE =   100
NUMBER OF MISSING VALUES    0   1   2   3   4
         NUMBER OF CASES   23  40  25  10   2
```

There are 23 cases with complete observations, 40 with one missing value, etc. If listwise deletion had been used, the effective sample size would have been 23. As the data matrix consists of 100 cases, this may seem like a very large reduction in the sample size. But this is actually typical of what will happen if 20 % (approximately 120 out of 600) of the data are missing at random.

EFFECTIVE SAMPLE SIZES
UNIVARIATE (IN DIAGONAL) AND PAIRWISE BIVARIATE (OFF DIAGONAL)
TOTAL SAMPLE SIZE = 100

	CONTIN1	ORDINAL1	ORDINAL2	ORDINAL3	CONTIN2	ORDINAL4
CONTIN1	79					
ORDINAL1	64	84				
ORDINAL2	60	63	78			
ORDINAL3	58	65	62	75		
CONTIN2	59	63	58	57	76	
ORDINAL4	65	67	64	60	62	80

There are 79 cases with no missing values on CONTIN1; 64 cases with no missing values on both CONTIN1 and ORDINAL1; etc. These are the effective sample sizes that will be used under pairwise deletion.

PERCENTAGE OF MISSING VALUES
UNIVARIATE (IN DIAGONAL) AND PAIRWISE BIVARIATE (OFF DIAGONAL)
TOTAL SAMPLE SIZE = 100

	CONTIN1	ORDINAL1	ORDINAL2	ORDINAL3	CONTIN2	ORDINAL4
CONTIN1	21.00					
ORDINAL1	36.00	16.00				
ORDINAL2	40.00	37.00	22.00			
ORDINAL3	42.00	35.00	38.00	25.00		
CONTIN2	41.00	37.00	42.00	43.00	24.00	
ORDINAL4	35.00	33.00	36.00	40.00	38.00	20.00

This table provides basically the same information as the previous table, but in terms of percentage of missing observations. Thus, 21 % of the 100 cases are missing on CONTIN1; 36 % are missing on both CONTIN1 and ORDINAL1; etc.

CONVERSION OF ORIGINAL VALUES TO CATEGORIES

VARIABLE	1	2	3	CATEGORY 4	5	6	7
ORDINAL1	1.00	2.00	3.00	4.00	5.00	6.00	7.00
ORDINAL2	1.00	2.00	3.00	4.00	5.00		
ORDINAL3	1.00	2.00	3.00				
ORDINAL4	1.00	2.00					

For each ordinal variable, this table shows which score values were found in the data and the categories to which the scores correspond.

UNIVARIATE FREQUENCY DISTRIBUTIONS FOR ORDINAL VARIABLES

VARIABLE	1	2	CATEGORY 3	4	5	6	7
ORDINAL1	4	15	6	6	11	17	25
ORDINAL2	28	14	6	9	21		
ORDINAL3	14	44	17				
ORDINAL4	24	56					

For each ordinal variable, this table gives the marginal frequency distribution. In this case, it is seen that ORDINAL1 has a skewed distribution, and ORDINAL2 has a U-shaped distribution.

CONTINGENCY TABLES FOR ORDINAL VARIABLES

	ORDINAL2					ORDINAL3			ORDINAL4	
ORDINAL1	1	2	3	4	5	1	2	3	1	2
1	2	0	1	0	0	1	1	0	2	1
2	6	1	0	0	2	3	9	1	8	3
3	3	1	0	1	1	0	2	1	3	3
4	2	2	0	0	1	3	2	1	0	2
5	2	4	0	1	1	2	5	1	2	7
6	5	0	2	3	4	2	8	3	2	11
7	4	3	2	1	8	0	12	8	5	18

	ORDINAL3			ORDINAL4	
ORDINAL2	1	2	3	1	2
1	8	10	2	7	15
2	4	6	3	4	9
3	0	4	2	3	1
4	0	4	2	0	6
5	0	9	8	2	17

	ORDINAL4	
ORDINAL3	1	2
1	4	7
2	11	24
3	3	11

This is a compact way of presenting contingency tables for all pairs of ordinal variables. Each contingency table is based on all cases with real observations of both variables. The sample sizes for each contingency table are those given by the off-diagonal elements in the table "Effective Sample Sizes" (described earlier).

UNIVARIATE SUMMARY STATISTICS FOR CONTINUOUS VARIABLES

VARIABLE	MEAN	ST DEV	SKEWNESS	KURTOSIS	MINIMUM	FREQ.	MAXIMUM	FREQ.
CONTIN1	-.011	1.189	-.040	-.566	-2.200	1	2.930	1
CONTIN2	-.164	1.082	-.215	-.060	-3.260	1	2.450	1

This table gives useful information about the marginal distribution of each continuous variable. The measures of skewness and kurtosis are γ_1 and γ_2 (see Kendall and Stuart, 1963, pp. 85–86), which are both zero for a normal distribution. To enable checking for clustering of observations at either end, the table also gives minimum and maximum values and their respective frequencies.

BIVARIATE SUMMARY STATISTICS FOR PAIRS OF VARIABLES WHERE THE FIRST VARIABLE IS ORDINAL AND THE SECOND IS CONTINUOUS

ORDINAL1 VS. CONTIN1

CATEGORY	NUMBER OF OBSERVATIONS	MEAN	STANDARD DEVIATION
1	4	-1.456	.224
2	11	-1.154	.928
3	4	-.151	.489
4	4	.411	.780
5	7	.347	.569
6	13	.402	.812
7	21	.807	.893

ORDINAL2 VS. CONTIN1

CATEGORY	NUMBER OF OBSERVATIONS	MEAN	STANDARD DEVIATION
1	21	-.487	1.109
2	12	-.091	1.207
3	5	.069	1.297
4	7	.157	.731
5	15	.582	1.361

ORDINAL3 VS. CONTIN1

CATEGORY	NUMBER OF OBSERVATIONS	MEAN	STANDARD DEVIATION
1	13	-.423	1.229
2	35	.015	1.165
3	10	.795	1.182

ORDINAL1 VS. CONTIN2

CATEGORY	NUMBER OF OBSERVATIONS	MEAN	STANDARD DEVIATION
1	3	-.630	1.299
2	11	-.036	.747
3	4	.114	1.217
4	4	-.071	1.089
5	8	-.060	1.138
6	13	-.072	.804
7	20	.397	1.055

ORDINAL2 VS. CONTIN2

CATEGORY	NUMBER OF OBSERVATIONS	MEAN	STANDARD DEVIATION
1	22	-.491	.919
2	9	.329	1.394
3	4	.399	.391
4	7	-.070	1.211
5	16	.260	.934

ORDINAL3 VS. CONTIN2

CATEGORY	NUMBER OF OBSERVATIONS	MEAN	STANDARD DEVIATION
1	7	-.969	1.603
2	35	.252	1.010
3	15	.189	.655

ORDINAL4 VS. CONTIN1

CATEGORY	NUMBER OF OBSERVATIONS	MEAN	STANDARD DEVIATION
1	20	-.345	1.414
2	45	.195	1.113

ORDINAL4 VS. CONTIN2

CATEGORY	NUMBER OF OBSERVATIONS	MEAN	STANDARD DEVIATION
1	20	.009	1.260
2	42	.085	.903

These tables give summary statistics for each pair of variables: one is ordinal, one is continuous. The table gives the mean and standard deviation of the continuous variable for each category of the ordinal variable. The overall mean of the continuous variable was subtracted from all the values before these summary statistics were computed.

CORRELATIONS AND TEST STATISTICS
(PE=PEARSON PRODUCT MOMENT, PC=POLYCHORIC, PS=POLYSERIAL)

	CORRELATION	TEST OF MODEL CHI-SQ.	D.F.	P-VALUE	TEST OF ZERO CORR. CHI-SQU.	P-VALUE
ORDINAL1 VS. CONTIN1	.681 (PS)	19.131	11	.059	42.153	.000
ORDINAL2 VS. CONTIN1	.355 (PS)	3.466	7	.839	7.856	.005
ORDINAL2 VS. ORDINAL1	.389 (PC)	23.831	23	.413	10.091	.000
ORDINAL3 VS. CONTIN1	.334 (PS)	.412	3	.938	6.618	.010
ORDINAL3 VS. ORDINAL1	.438 (PC)	8.745	11	.645	13.680	.000
ORDINAL3 VS. ORDINAL2	.562 (PC)	6.187	7	.518	23.814	.000
CONTIN2 VS. CONTIN1	.248 (PE)				3.604	.058
ORDINAL1 VS. CONTIN2	.214 (PS)	5.621	11	.897	2.836	.092
ORDINAL2 VS. CONTIN2	.280 (PS)	10.543	7	.160	4.555	.033
ORDINAL3 VS. CONTIN2	.259 (PS)	13.194	3	.004	3.802	.051
ORDINAL4 VS. CONTIN1	.249 (PS)	1.826	1	.177	4.017	.045
ORDINAL4 VS. ORDINAL1	.473 (PC)	6.369	5	.272	16.881	.000
ORDINAL4 VS. ORDINAL2	.310 (PC)	8.365	3	.039	6.255	.012
ORDINAL4 VS. ORDINAL3	.160 (PC)	.061	1	.804	1.487	.223
ORDINAL4 VS. CONTIN2	.042 (PS)	3.246	1	.072	.103	.748

For each pair of variables for which a polychoric or polyserial correlation has been estimated, this table provides a goodness-of-fit test of the model of an underlying bivariate normal distribution. Such a test is not provided when the estimated correlation is a product moment correlation; neither is such a test possible for the tetrachoric correlation coefficient between two dichotomous variables. The table also gives statistics for testing the hypothesis that the correlation in the bivariate normal distribution is zero.

ESTIMATED CORRELATION MATRIX

	CONTIN1	ORDINAL1	ORDINAL2	ORDINAL3	CONTIN2	ORDINAL4
CONTIN1	1.000					
ORDINAL1	.681	1.000				
ORDINAL2	.355	.389	1.000			
ORDINAL3	.334	.438	.562	1.000		
CONTIN2	.248	.214	.280	.259	1.000	
ORDINAL4	.249	.473	.310	.160	.042	1.000

This correlation matrix may be saved in a file by specifying `MATRIX = OUT (file)`.

Computer Exercise 1

Run the same data using the `TYPE=CORR` and `TYPE=AUGMENTED` options. Compare the correlations.

Logarithmic Transformations and Recoding Variables

As a variation of the previous example, in Example 1B we transform CONTIN1 by a logarithmic transformation

$$y = \log(3 + x)$$

and dichotomize ORDINAL1 and ORDINAL2 as evenly as possible. For the transformed data, we compute the matrix of product moment correlations using normal scores for the ordinal variables. This time we use listwise deletion.

```
TITLE "PRELIS test on artificial data; 1B"
DATA LIST FILE=file FREE
 /1 CONTIN1 ORDINAL1 ORDINAL2 ORDINAL3
    CONTIN2 ORDINAL4
MISSING VALUES CONTIN1 TO ORDINAL4 (-9)
COMPUTE CONTIN1 = LN(3 + CONTIN1)
RECODE ORDINAL1 (1 THRU 5 = 0) (6 THRU 7 = 1)
RECODE ORDINAL2 (1 THRU 2 = 0) (3 THRU 5 = 1)
```

```
PRELIS
   /VARIABLES = CONTIN1 (CO) ORDINAL1 TO ORDINAL3 (OR)
                CONTIN2 (CO) ORDINAL4 (OR)
   /MISSING   = LISTWISE EXCLUDE
   /TYPE      = CORR
   /MATRIX    = NONE
FINISH
```

The log transformation of CONTIN1 is safe because we found in the previous run that the smallest observed value on CONTIN1 was −2.2. Both ORDINAL1 and ORDINAL2 were dichotomized using the SPSS RECODE command.

```
DISTRIBUTION OF MISSING VALUES
TOTAL SAMPLE SIZE =  23

NUMBER OF MISSING VALUES   0   1   2   3   4
         NUMBER OF CASES  23  40  25  10   2
```

Of the 100 cases, there are only 23 with complete data on all variables. MISSING=LISTWISE, so 23 will be the sample size in this run.

```
LISTWISE DELETION
TOTAL EFFECTIVE SAMPLE SIZE =  23

CONVERSION OF ORIGINAL VALUES TO CATEGORIES
```

VARIABLE	CATEGORY 1	2	3
ORDINAL1	.00	1.00	
ORDINAL2	.00	1.00	
ORDINAL3	1.00	2.00	3.00
ORDINAL4	1.00	2.00	

Note that ORDINAL1 and ORDINAL2 have now been dichotomized and have scores 0 and 1 only.

UNIVARIATE FREQUENCY DISTRIBUTIONS FOR ORDINAL VARIABLES

VARIABLE	CATEGORY 1	2	3
ORDINAL1	8	15	
ORDINAL2	11	12	
ORDINAL3	3	15	5
ORDINAL4	6	17	

These are the distributions in the listwise sample after ORDINAL1 and ORDINAL2 have been dichotomized.

NORMAL SCORES FOR ORDINAL VARIABLES

VARIABLE	CATEGORY 1	2	3
ORDINAL1	-1.062	.567	
ORDINAL2	-.833	.764	
ORDINAL3	-1.626	-.126	1.353
ORDINAL4	-1.246	.440	

These normal scores replace the ordinal data when the correlations (TYPE=CORR) are computed.

UNIVARIATE SUMMARY STATISTICS FOR CONTINUOUS VARIABLES

VARIABLE	MEAN	ST.DEV.	SKEWNESS	KURTOSIS	MINIMUM	FREQ.	MAXIMUM	FREQ.
CONTIN1	1.012	.464	-.890	-.021	-.062	1	1.651	1
CONTIN2	-.118	.884	-.161	-.350	-1.960	1	1.510	1

These summary statistics are for the listwise sample and after CONTIN1 has been transformed.

ESTIMATED CORRELATION MATRIX

	CONTIN1	ORDINAL1	ORDINAL2	ORDINAL3	CONTIN2	ORDINAL4
CONTIN1	1.000					
ORDINAL1	.461	1.000				
ORDINAL2	.139	.215	1.000			
ORDINAL3	.137	.421	.442	1.000		
CONTIN2	.061	-.205	.394	.121	1.000	
ORDINAL4	.407	.606	.224	.089	-.286	1.000

Select Cases, Estimate Augmented Moment Matrix

As a second variation of the first example, in Example 1C we use the original 100 observations and select those cases which have values larger than zero on CONTIN1 (cases with missing values were included as well, to make comparison with the stand-alone version output easy). For these cases, we estimate the augmented moment matrix.

```
TITLE "PRELIS test on artificial data; 1C"
DATA LIST FILE=file FREE
 /1 CONTIN1 ORDINAL1 ORDINAL2 ORDINAL3
    CONTIN2 ORDINAL4
MISSING VALUES CONTIN1 TO ORDINAL4 (-9)
SELECT IF (CONTIN1 GT 0 OR MISSING(CONTIN1))
PRELIS CONTIN1 (CO) ORDINAL1 TO ORDINAL3 (OR)
       CONTIN2 (CO) ORDINAL4 (OR)
   /MISSING    = PAIRWISE EXCLUDE
   /TYPE       = AUGMENTED
   /MATRIX     = NONE
FINISH
```

```
DISTRIBUTION OF MISSING VALUES
TOTAL SAMPLE SIZE =     65
NUMBER OF MISSING VALUES    0   1   2   3   4
         NUMBER OF CASES   13  28  15   8   1
```

The total selected subsample is 65, but it includes cases with missing values. In this run, pairwise deletion is used in the selected subsample.

EFFECTIVE SAMPLE SIZES
UNIVARIATE (IN DIAGONAL) AND PAIRWISE BIVARIATE (OFF DIAGONAL)
TOTAL SAMPLE SIZE = 65

	CONTIN1	ORDINAL1	ORDINAL2	ORDINAL3	CONTIN2	ORDINAL4
CONTIN1	44					
ORDINAL1	39	59				
ORDINAL2	34	46	52			
ORDINAL3	33	47	44	50		
CONTIN2	30	43	36	36	47	
ORDINAL4	37	46	42	38	39	52

PERCENTAGE OF MISSING VALUES
UNIVARIATE (IN DIAGONAL) AND PAIRWISE BIVARIATE (OFF DIAGONAL)
TOTAL SAMPLE SIZE = 65

	CONTIN1	ORDINAL1	ORDINAL2	ORDINAL3	CONTIN2	ORDINAL4
CONTIN1	32.31					
ORDINAL1	40.00	9.23				
ORDINAL2	47.69	29.23	20.00			
ORDINAL3	49.23	27.69	32.31	23.08		
CONTIN2	53.85	33.85	44.62	44.62	27.69	
ORDINAL4	43.08	29.23	35.38	41.54	40.00	20.00

CONVERSION OF ORIGINAL VALUES TO CATEGORIES

VARIABLE	CATEGORY 1	2	3	4	5	6
ORDINAL1	2.00	3.00	4.00	5.00	6.00	7.00
ORDINAL2	1.00	2.00	3.00	4.00	5.00	
ORDINAL3	1.00	2.00	3.00			
ORDINAL4	1.00	2.00				

UNIVARIATE FREQUENCY DISTRIBUTIONS FOR ORDINAL VARIABLES

VARIABLE	CATEGORY 1	2	3	4	5	6
ORDINAL1	5	4	5	10	15	20
ORDINAL2	17	8	3	7	17	
ORDINAL3	8	28	14			
ORDINAL4	12	40				

These are the distributions of ordinal variables in the subsample selected on CONTIN1.

NORMAL SCORES FOR ORDINAL VARIABLES

VARIABLE	CATEGORY 1	2	3	4	5	6
ORDINAL1	-1.832	-1.188	-.863	-.466	.087	1.080
ORDINAL2	-1.104	-.245	.024	.270	1.104	
ORDINAL3	-1.521	-.167	1.202			
ORDINAL4	-1.318	.395				

UNIVARIATE SUMMARY STATISTICS FOR CONTINUOUS VARIABLES

VARIABLE	MEAN	ST.DEV.	SKEWNESS	KURTOSIS	MINIMUM	FREQ.	MAXIMUM	FREQ.
CONTIN1	.858	.667	1.143	.915	.020	1	2.930	1
CONTIN2	-.023	1.012	-.090	-.809	-1.960	1	1.720	1

These are summary statistics for the subsample of cases with positive values of CONTIN1.

ESTIMATED AUGMENTED MOMENT MATRIX

	CONTIN1	ORDINAL1	ORDINAL2	ORDINAL3	CONTIN2	ORDINAL4	CONST.
CONTIN1	1.171						
ORDINAL1	.424	.877					
ORDINAL2	.258	.245	.815				
ORDINAL3	.065	.199	.384	.790			
CONTIN2	.106	.294	.227	.094	1.003		
ORDINAL4	-.043	.175	.024	-.035	-.015	.521	
CONST.	.858	.000	.000	.000	-.023	.000	1.000

The last row of the augmented moment matrix contains means of variables in the selected subsample. Note that means are zero for ordinal variables because the means of their normal scores are zero.

Polychoric Correlations Matrix with All Variables Ordinal

Swedish school children in grade 9 were asked questions about their attitudes on social issues in family, school, and society. Among the questions asked were the following eight items [in free translation from Swedish] (Hasselrot & Lernberg, 1980).

For me, questions about ...

1. human rights
2. equal conditions for all people
3. racial problems
4. equal value of all people

5. euthanasia
6. crime and punishment
7. conscientious objectors
8. guilt and bad conscience

are:
___unimportant ___not important ___important ___very important

For Example 2, we use a subsample of 200 cases. Responses to the eight questions were scored 1, 2, 3, and 4 (4 = very important). Missing values were scored zero. The data matrix consists of 200 rows and 8 columns.

```
TITLE "Attitudes of Morality and Equality"
DATA LIST FILE=file FIXED RECORDS=1
 /1 HUMRGHTS 1 EQUALCON 2 RACEPROB 3 EQUALVAL 4
    EUTHANAS 5 CRIMEPUN 6 CONSCOBJ 7 GUILT    8
MISSING VALUES HUMRGHTS TO GUILT (0)
PRELIS
   /VARIABLES = HUMRGHTS TO GUILT (OR)
   /MISSING   = PAIRWISE EXCLUDE
   /TYPE      = POLYCHORIC
   /MATRIX    = NONE
FINISH
```

```
DISTRIBUTION OF MISSING VALUES
TOTAL SAMPLE SIZE =  200
NUMBER OF MISSING VALUES   0   1   2   3
         NUMBER OF CASES 195   4   0   1
```

There are only five cases with missing values!

(Three sections of the output have been skipped at this point.)

UNIVARIATE FREQUENCY DISTRIBUTIONS FOR ORDINAL VARIABLES

VARIABLE	CATEGORY 1	2	3	4
HUMRGHTS	3	12	73	110
EQUALCON	5	25	86	83
RACEPROB	15	17	85	80
EQUALVAL	10	46	68	76
EUTHANAS	7	23	77	93
CRIMEPUN	2	26	99	73
CONSCOBJ	39	51	78	32
GUILT	15	40	104	40

All of the variables except the last two are highly skewed.

CONTINGENCY TABLES FOR ORDINAL VARIABLES

	EQUALCON				RACEPROB				EQUALVAL				EUTHANAS			
HUMRGHTS	1	2	3	4	1	2	3	4	1	2	3	4	1	2	3	4
1	0	0	2	1	2	0	0	1	0	0	2	1	0	0	2	1
2	3	4	4	1	0	2	7	3	3	6	3	0	3	4	4	1
3	0	13	39	21	6	7	36	24	2	24	28	19	2	9	40	22
4	2	7	41	60	7	8	41	52	5	16	34	55	2	9	31	68

HUMRGHTS	CRIMEPUN 1	2	3	4	CONSCOBJ 1	2	3	4	GUILT 1	2	3	4
1	0	0	1	2	0	1	1	1	1	0	0	2
2	0	5	6	1	6	4	1	1	3	4	4	1
3	0	11	41	21	13	22	31	7	2	14	44	12
4	2	10	50	48	20	24	43	23	8	22	55	25

Only a few of the contingency tables are given here. These show, for example, that of the 110 students who think that human rights are very important, 60 think that equal conditions are also very important.

CORRELATIONS AND TEST STATISTICS
(PE=PEARSON PRODUCT MOMENT, PC=POLYCHORIC, PS=POLYSERIAL)

	CORRELATION	TEST OF MODEL CHI-SQU.	DF	P-VALUE	TEST OF ZERO CORR. CHI-SQU.	P-VALUE
EQUALCON VS HUMRGHTS	.418 (PC)	14.708	8	.065	38.666	.000
RACEPROB VS HUMRGHTS	.221 (PC)	10.872	8	.209	9.745	.002
RACEPROB VS EQUALCON	.202 (PC)	4.933	8	.765	8.135	.004
EQUALVAL VS HUMRGHTS	.373 (PC)	16.735	8	.033	29.989	.000
EQUALVAL VS EQUALCON	.635 (PC)	13.097	8	.109	110.132	.000
EQUALVAL VS RACEPROB	.285 (PC)	10.408	8	.238	16.695	.000
EUTHANAS VS HUMRGHTS	.442 (PC)	12.341	8	.137	43.943	.000
EUTHANAS VS EQUALCON	.706 (PC)	9.872	8	.274	151.517	.000
EUTHANAS VS RACEPROB	.317 (PC)	7.348	8	.500	20.890	.000
EUTHANAS VS EQUALVAL	.692 (PC)	26.238	8	.001	142.610	.000
CRIMEPUN VS HUMRGHTS	.215 (PC)	12.460	8	.132	9.328	.002
CRIMEPUN VS EQUALCON	.236 (PC)	17.785	8	.023	11.352	.000
CRIMEPUN VS RACEPROB	.282 (PC)	14.366	8	.073	16.287	.000
CRIMEPUN VS EQUALVAL	.423 (PC)	13.672	8	.091	40.183	.000
CRIMEPUN VS EUTHANAS	.218 (PC)	13.103	8	.108	9.690	.002
CONSCOBJ VS HUMRGHTS	.190 (PC)	11.504	8	.175	7.199	.007
CONSCOBJ VS EQUALCON	.292 (PC)	10.694	8	.220	17.777	.000
CONSCOBJ VS RACEPROB	.312 (PC)	6.467	8	.595	20.238	.000
CONSCOBJ VS EQUALVAL	.340 (PC)	14.912	8	.061	24.699	.000
CONSCOBJ VS EUTHANAS	.224 (PC)	7.263	8	.509	10.225	.000
CONSCOBJ VS CRIMEPUN	.312 (PC)	9.113	8	.333	20.578	.000
GUILT VS HUMRGHTS	.094 (PC)	17.361	8	.027	1.719	.190
GUILT VS EQUALCON	.314 (PC)	15.453	8	.051	20.656	.000
GUILT VS RACEPROB	.239 (PC)	8.626	8	.375	11.466	.000
GUILT VS EQUALVAL	.320 (PC)	7.392	8	.495	21.523	.000
GUILT VS EUTHANAS	.340 (PC)	8.500	8	.386	24.618	.000
GUILT VS CRIMEPUN	.207 (PC)	7.595	8	.474	8.606	.003
GUILT VS CONSCOBJ	.202 (PC)	12.879	8	.116	8.202	.004

Despite the fact that most of the marginal distributions are highly skewed, only 1 out of 28 of the model tests reject the hypothesis of an underlying bivariate normal distribution at the 1 % nominal level of significance. When examining many tests like this, bear in mind that if all the hypotheses were true, a 1 % long-run rejection rate should be expected by pure chance.

ESTIMATED CORRELATION MATRIX

	HUMRGHTS	EQUALCON	RACEPROB	EQUALVAL	EUTHANAS	CRIMEPUN
HUMRGHTS	1.000					
EQUALCON	.418	1.000				
RACEPROB	.221	.202	1.000			
EQUALVAL	.373	.635	.285	1.000		
EUTHANAS	.442	.706	.317	.692	1.000	
CRIMEPUN	.215	.236	.282	.423	.218	1.000
CONSCOBJ	.190	.292	.312	.340	.224	.312
GUILT	.094	.314	.239	.320	.340	.207

ESTIMATED CORRELATION MATRIX

	CONSCOBJ	GUILT
CONSCOBJ	1.000	
GUILT	.202	1.000

Computer Exercise 2

Run the same data using the `TYPE = CORRELATION` or `TYPE = OPTIMAL` subcommands. Compare the correlations.

Censored Variables

The next data file consists of scores of Swedish school children on reading and spelling tests that relate to metaphonological aspects of the Swedish language. Each score is the number of correctly answered items. There are 11 tests and 90 cases. In the first run (Example 3A), we treat all variables as continuous and estimate the product-moment correlations. In the second run (Example 3B), after observing that some of the tests have large "floor" and "ceiling" effects, we declare all variables as censored and re-estimate the product-moment correlations.

```
TITLE "Example 3A: Test Score Data"
DATA LIST FILE=file FREE
   /1 V01 V02 V07 V08 V09 V10 V21 V22 V23 V24 V25
PRELIS V01 TO V25 (CO)
   /TYPE=CORR /PRI=NONE /MATRIX=NONE
```

In Example 3A, all variables are continuous.

UNIVARIATE SUMMARY STATISTICS FOR CONTINUOUS VARIABLES

VARIABLE	MEAN	ST.DEV.	SKEWNESS	KURTOSIS	MINIMUM	FREQ.	MAXIMUM	FREQ.
V01	21.789	7.856	-1.117	.324	.000	2	30.000	6
V02	14.622	7.048	-.173	-.548	.000	2	28.000	5
V07	11.489	3.069	-.175	2.587	.000	1	20.000	2
V08	14.478	3.660	-.490	2.852	.000	1	25.000	1
V09	19.122	6.830	-.635	.349	.000	3	32.000	1
V10	21.622	5.560	-.553	.160	6.000	1	33.000	2
V21	15.022	2.998	-1.956	3.314	4.000	1	17.000	41
V22	13.122	3.304	-1.123	.906	2.000	1	17.000	8
V23	12.578	3.402	-1.141	.713	3.000	3	16.000	21
V24	8.611	3.550	-.271	-.531	.000	1	15.000	2
V25	16.589	4.271	-1.338	2.347	1.000	1	22.000	9

V21 has a high negative skewness; V07, V08, V21, and V25 have high kurtoses; and V21 and V23 have high ceiling effects. Obviously, V21 is a very problematic variable. For data like these, it is likely that the correlations will be biased due to restrictions of range.

ESTIMATED CORRELATION MATRIX

	V01	V02	V07	V08	V09	V10	V21	V22	V23	V24	V25
V01	1.000										
V02	.755	1.000									
V07	.634	.599	1.000								
V08	.640	.618	.872	1.000							
V09	.474	.429	.345	.377	1.000						
V10	.309	.423	.339	.330	.581	1.000					
V21	.554	.568	.393	.423	.296	.322	1.000				
V22	.509	.527	.434	.399	.309	.360	.625	1.000			
V23	.518	.596	.484	.474	.425	.489	.564	.519	1.000		
V24	.662	.672	.603	.569	.503	.529	.538	.613	.558	1.000	
V25	.726	.756	.528	.516	.380	.397	.731	.634	.619	.628	1.000

In the second run, Example 3B, we treat all variables as censored below and above. The word CENSORED may be abbreviated to **CE**.

```
TITLE "Example 3B: Test Score Data"
DATA LIST FILE=file FREE
   /1 V01 V02 V07 V08 V09 V10 V21 V22 V23 V24 V25
PRELIS V01 TO V25 (CENSORED)
   /TYPE=CORR /PRI=NONE /MATRIX=NONE
```

UNIVARIATE SUMMARY STATISTICS FOR CONTINUOUS VARIABLES

VARIABLE	MEAN	ST.DEV.	SKEWNESS	KURTOSIS	MINIMUM	FREQ.	MAXIMUM	FREQ.
V01	22.031	8.411	-.987	.545	-2.628	2	34.506	6
V02	14.727	7.536	-.032	-.051	-2.853	2	31.032	5
V07	11.502	3.165	-.119	3.198	-.772	1	20.972	2
V08	14.480	3.737	-.500	3.433	-.865	1	26.109	1
V09	19.081	7.108	-.748	.976	-2.182	3	34.808	1
V10	21.651	5.723	-.487	.524	4.266	1	35.147	2
V21	16.444	4.191	-1.059	.706	2.804	1	20.150	41
V22	13.275	3.569	-.861	.928	1.028	1	18.844	8
V23	13.116	4.216	-.656	.332	1.600	3	18.506	21
V24	8.630	3.650	-.233	-.253	-1.224	1	16.476	2
V25	16.810	4.665	-.966	2.044	-.203	1	24.349	9

Both skewness and kurtosis are now smaller than before for all variables but V07 and V08, and the maximum and minimum values have been moved further out.

ESTIMATED CORRELATION MATRIX

	V01	V02	V07	V08	V09	V10	V21	V22	V23	V24	V25
V01	1.000										
V02	.759	1.000									
V07	.649	.605	1.000								
V08	.637	.610	.873	1.000							
V09	.484	.421	.355	.373	1.000						
V10	.315	.431	.344	.320	.563	1.000					
V21	.558	.579	.446	.464	.345	.336	1.000				
V22	.515	.545	.431	.399	.300	.361	.590	1.000			
V23	.505	.584	.487	.457	.438	.483	.536	.487	1.000		
V24	.674	.693	.613	.570	.497	.535	.532	.632	.552	1.000	
V25	.715	.768	.541	.515	.387	.417	.692	.637	.615	.644	1.000

Many correlations in this table are smaller than in the previous run, especially those for variables V21 and V23.

Tetrachoric Correlations, with Asymptotic Variances Estimated from Grouped Data

Bock and Lieberman (1970) and Christoffersson (1975) published the data in Table 1 on the next page: observed frequencies for the 32 response patterns arising from five items (11 through 15) of Section 6 of the Law School Admissions Test (LSAT). All items are dichotomous.

The sample is a subsample of 1000 from a larger sample of those who took the test. In Example 4, we use this data to illustrate how fast SPSS PRELIS can compute tetrachoric correlations for these five items and asymptotic variances of these correlations.

```
TITLE "Example 4: LSAT Section 6"
DATA LIST FILE=file FREE
   /1 VAR1 VAR2 VAR3 VAR4 VAR5 VAR6
WEIGHT BY VAR6
PRELIS VAR1 TO VAR5 (OR)
   /TYPE    = POLY
   /MATRIX = NONE
   /WRITE   = AVAR file
   /PRINT   = AVAR
```

Some sections of the output follow.

UNIVARIATE FREQUENCY DISTRIBUTIONS FOR ORDINAL VARIABLES

VARIABLE	CATEGORY 1	2
VAR 1	76	924
VAR 2	291	709
VAR 3	447	553
VAR 4	237	763
VAR 5	130	870

Table 1

Observed Frequencies of Response Patterns for Five Items of LSAT6

Pattern Index	Item 1	2	3	4	5	Frequency
1	0	0	0	0	0	3
2	0	0	0	0	1	6
3	0	0	0	1	0	2
4	0	0	0	1	1	11
5	0	0	1	0	0	1
6	0	0	1	0	1	1
7	0	0	1	1	0	3
8	0	0	1	1	1	4
9	0	1	0	0	0	1
10	0	1	0	0	1	8
11	0	1	0	1	0	0
12	0	1	0	1	1	16
13	0	1	1	0	0	0
14	0	1	1	0	1	3
15	0	1	1	1	0	2
16	0	1	1	1	1	15
17	1	0	0	0	0	10
18	1	0	0	0	1	29
19	1	0	0	1	0	14
20	1	0	0	1	1	81
21	1	0	1	0	0	3
22	1	0	1	0	1	28
23	1	0	1	1	0	15
24	1	0	1	1	1	80
25	1	1	0	0	0	16
26	1	1	0	0	1	56
27	1	1	0	1	0	21
28	1	1	0	1	1	173
29	1	1	1	0	0	11
30	1	1	1	0	1	61
31	1	1	1	1	0	28
32	1	1	1	1	1	298
				Total		1000

CONTINGENCY TABLES FOR ORDINAL VARIABLES

VAR 1	VAR 2: 1	VAR 2: 2	VAR 3: 1	VAR 3: 2	VAR 4: 1	VAR 4: 2	VAR 5: 1	VAR 5: 2
1	31	45	47	29	23	53	12	64
2	260	664	400	524	214	710	118	806

VAR 2	VAR 3: 1	VAR 3: 2	VAR 4: 1	VAR 4: 2	VAR 5: 1	VAR 5: 2
1	156	135	81	210	51	240
2	291	418	156	553	79	630

VAR 3	VAR 4: 1	VAR 4: 2	VAR 5: 1	VAR 5: 2
1	129	318	67	380
2	108	445	63	490

VAR 4	VAR 5: 1	VAR 5: 2
1	45	192
2	85	678

The joint occurrence proportions (proportions of examinees who give correct answers to both items) for each pair of variables can be extracted easily from these tables.

ESTIMATED CORRELATION MATRIX

	VAR 1	VAR 2	VAR 3	VAR 4	VAR 5
VAR 1	1.000				
VAR 2	.170	1.000			
VAR 3	.228	.189	1.000		
VAR 4	.107	.111	.187	1.000	
VAR 5	.067	.172	.105	.201	1.000

These correlations essentially agree with those reported by Christoffersson (1975). The largest difference is two units in the third decimal.

ASYMPTOTIC VARIANCES OF ESTIMATED CORRELATIONS

R(2,1)	R(3,1)	R(3,2)	R(4,1)	R(4,2)	R(4,3)
.00549	.00504	.00263	.00611	.00322	.00284

R(5,1)	R(5,2)	R(5,3)	R(5,4)
.00819	.00408	.00392	.00425

These are large sample estimates of the variances of the estimated tetrachoric correlations. The square roots of these variances are the standard errors of the estimated correlations. These can be used to set up approximate confidence intervals for the correlations. For example, an approximate 95 % confidence interval for ρ_{21} is $.170 \pm 2\surd\ .00549 = .170 \pm .148$.

Estimating Asymptotic Variances and Covariances (a)

Examples 5A, 5B, and 5C illustrate how to obtain estimates of asymptotic variances and covariances of the estimated variances, covariances, or correlations between the variables. They are based on generated data consisting of 200 cases on five variables, where the first two variables are continuous and the last three are ordinal. Variables 3, 4, and 5 have 2, 3, and 4 categories, respectively. The data were generated from a population in which all variances were 1.0 and all intercorrelations were 0.5. The output files produced in these examples are files where the asymptotic covariance matrices are stored. These can be read directly by LISREL 7 and used with the WLS option.

In Example 5A, we estimate (1) variances and covariances of the variables using normal scores for the ordinal variables, (2) the asymptotic covariance matrix of these variances and covariances, and (3) the relative multivariate kurtosis. Complete output for this example follows.

```
TITLE "Asymptotic Variances and Covariances, 5A"
DATA LIST FILE=file FREE
   /1 VAR1 VAR2 VAR3 VAR4 VAR5
PRELIS
   /MAXCAT = 4
   /VAR    = VAR1 VAR2 (CONTINUOUS)
             VAR3 TO VAR5 (ORDINAL)
   /TYPE   = COVARIANCE /MATRIX = NONE
   /PRINT  = ACOV,KURTOSIS
   /WRITE  = ACOV file
```

TOTAL SAMPLE SIZE = 200

CONVERSION OF ORIGINAL VALUES TO CATEGORIES

VARIABLE	CATEGORY 1	2	3	4
VAR 3	1.00	2.00		
VAR 4	1.00	2.00	3.00	
VAR 5	1.00	2.00	3.00	4.00

UNIVARIATE FREQUENCY DISTRIBUTIONS FOR ORDINAL VARIABLES

VARIABLE	CATEGORY 1	2	3	4
VAR 3	88	112		
VAR 4	46	74	80	
VAR 5	42	43	51	64

NORMAL SCORES FOR ORDINAL VARIABLES

VARIABLE	CATEGORY 1	2	3	4
VAR 3	-.896	.704		
VAR 4	-1.320	-.223	.966	
VAR 5	-1.372	-.482	.134	1.118

UNIVARIATE SUMMARY STATISTICS FOR CONTINUOUS VARIABLES

VARIABLE	MEAN	ST.DEV.	SKEWNESS	KURTOSIS	MINIMUM	FREQ.	MAXIMUM	FREQ.
VAR 1	.084	1.042	.035	.051	-2.920	1	3.040	1
VAR 2	.010	1.015	.166	.860	-2.850	1	4.060	1

ESTIMATED COVARIANCE MATRIX

	VAR 1	VAR 2	VAR 3	VAR 4	VAR 5
VAR 1	1.086				
VAR 2	.498	1.030			
VAR 3	.328	.314	.635		
VAR 4	.394	.319	.287	.796	
VAR 5	.443	.424	.297	.364	.854

RELATIVE MULTIVARIATE KURTOSIS = .923909D+00

ASYMPTOTIC COVARIANCE MATRIX OF ESTIMATED VARIANCES AND COVARIANCES

	S(1,1)	S(2,1)	S(2,2)	S(3,1)	S(3,2)	S(3,3)
S(1,1)	.01179					
S(2,1)	.00368	.00642				
S(2,2)	.00211	.00704	.01482			
S(3,1)	.00292	.00164	.00080	.00282		
S(3,2)	.00076	.00170	.00302	.00106	.00270	
S(3,3)	-.00005	.00000	-.00005	.00006	.00006	.00012
S(4,1)	.00489	.00237	.00162	.00149	.00049	.00007
S(4,2)	.00163	.00284	.00444	.00059	.00145	.00004
S(4,3)	.00059	.00040	.00049	.00084	.00059	.00005

S(4,4)	.00113	.00027	.00039	.00021	.00001	.00004
S(5,1)	.00481	.00238	.00190	.00156	.00036	.00006
S(5,2)	.00119	.00312	.00519	.00036	.00136	-.00006
S(5,3)	.00068	.00031	.00051	.00097	.00081	.00005
S(5,4)	.00172	.00077	.00124	.00029	.00030	.00002
S(5,5)	.00080	.00027	.00060	.00000	.00015	.00005

ASYMPTOTIC COVARIANCE MATRIX OF ESTIMATED VARIANCES AND COVARIANCES

	S(4,1)	S(4,2)	S(4,3)	S(4,4)	S(5,1)	S(5,2)
S(4,1)	.00465					
S(4,2)	.00161	.00395				
S(4,3)	.00095	.00079	.00214			
S(4,4)	.00118	.00097	.00070	.00210		
S(5,1)	.00282	.00097	.00025	.00049	.00442	
S(5,2)	.00084	.00243	.00026	.00018	.00145	.00407
S(5,3)	.00030	.00040	.00075	.00008	.00074	.00085
S(5,4)	.00153	.00128	.00073	.00091	.00145	.00122
S(5,5)	.00059	.00063	-.00006	.00051	.00129	.00120

ASYMPTOTIC COVARIANCE MATRIX OF ESTIMATED VARIANCES AND COVARIANCES

	S(5,3)	S(5,4)	S(5,5)
S(5,3)	.00229		
S(5,4)	.00062	.00322	
S(5,5)	.00077	.00103	.00267

The covariance matrix has 15 independent elements, so the asymptotic covariance matrix of these 15 elements is a symmetric matrix of order 15 by 15.

The lower half of this matrix, including the diagonal, contains 15 × 16/2 elements and is printed in sections. The matrix stored in the file named in the `WRITE` subcommand is equal to N times the asymptotic covariance printed in the output (N is the sample size; in this case, N=200). It is written in lines of 6 numbers, each in the format 6D13.6.

To obtain WLS estimates with LISREL 7, one need only include the subcommand line `AC FI=file` in the LISREL command file.

Estimating Asymptotic Variances and Covariances (b)

In Example 5B, we estimate the correlations of the variables, still using normal scores for the ordinal variables, and the asymptotic covariance matrix of these correlations. Here, we give only those parts of the output which differ from the previous example.

ESTIMATED CORRELATION MATRIX

	VAR 1	VAR 2	VAR 3	VAR 4	VAR 5
VAR 1	1.000				
VAR 2	.471	1.000			
VAR 3	.395	.388	1.000		
VAR 4	.424	.352	.403	1.000	
VAR 5	.460	.452	.403	.442	1.000

ASYMPTOTIC COVARIANCE MATRIX OF ESTIMATED CORRELATIONS

	R(2,1)	R(3,1)	R(3,2)	R(4,1)	R(4,2)	R(4,3)
R(2,1)	.00308					
R(3,1)	.00068	.00211				
R(3,2)	.00021	.00081	.00206			
R(4,1)	.00077	.00039	.00011	.00280		
R(4,2)	.00089	.00019	.00057	.00078	.00259	
R(4,3)	.00016	.00071	.00050	.00056	.00047	.00193
R(5,1)	.00072	.00049	-.00011	.00113	.00021	.00010
R(5,2)	.00094	.00008	.00033	.00024	.00099	.00018
R(5,3)	.00004	.00084	.00069	.00007	.00020	.00075
R(5,4)	.00011	-.00001	.00007	.00080	.00069	.00052

ASYMPTOTIC COVARIANCE MATRIX OF ESTIMATED CORRELATIONS

	R(5,1)	R(5,2)	R(5,3)	R(5,4)
R(5,1)	.00247			
R(5,2)	.00050	.00213		
R(5,3)	.00029	.00048	.00208	
R(5,4)	.00069	.00061	.00036	.00265

The correlation matrix has 10 estimated correlations, so the asymptotic covariance matrix of these has $.5 \times 10 \times 11 = 55$ independent elements. Note that the variances of the correlations are smaller than the variances of the corresponding covariances.

Estimating Asymptotic Variances and Covariances (c)

In Example 5C, we use the **TYPE=POLYCHOR** subcommand to estimate polychoric and polyserial correlations between the variables, and the asymptotic variances and covariances of these. We give only the parts of the output which differ from the previous two examples.

```
CONTINGENCY TABLES FOR ORDINAL VARIABLES

              VAR 4          VAR 5
          ------------  ----------------
  VAR 3    1   2   3    1   2   3   4
--------  ------------  ----------------
  1       33  38  17   30  28  16  14
  2       13  36  63   12  15  35  50

                 VAR 5
          ----------------
  VAR 4    1   2   3   4
--------  ----------------
  1       21  11   8   6
  2       13  25  21  15
  3        8   7  22  43

BIVARIATE SUMMARY STATISTICS FOR PAIRS OF VARIABLES WHERE
THE FIRST VARIABLE IS ORDINAL AND THE SECOND IS CONTINUOUS

  VAR 3 VS.   VAR 1
  --------   -------
CATEGORY   NUMBER OF OBSERVATIONS   MEAN  STANDARD DEVIATION
--------   ----------------------   ----  ------------------
  1                   88           -.463         .892
  2                  112            .364        1.010

  VAR 3 VS.   VAR 2
  --------   -------
CATEGORY   NUMBER OF OBSERVATIONS   MEAN  STANDARD DEVIATION
--------   ----------------------   ----  ------------------
  1                   88           -.443         .872
  2                  112            .348         .986

  VAR 4 VS.   VAR 1
  --------   -------
CATEGORY   NUMBER OF OBSERVATIONS   MEAN  STANDARD DEVIATION
--------   ----------------------   ----  ------------------
  1                   46           -.736        1.071
  2                   74           -.012         .854
  3                   80            .434         .950

  VAR 4 VS.   VAR 2
  --------   -------
CATEGORY   NUMBER OF OBSERVATIONS   MEAN  STANDARD DEVIATION
--------   ----------------------   ----  ------------------
  1                   46           -.604         .928
  2                   74            .000         .950
  3                   80            .347         .967

  VAR 5 VS.   VAR 1
  --------   -------
CATEGORY   NUMBER OF OBSERVATIONS   MEAN  STANDARD DEVIATION
--------   ----------------------   ----  ------------------
  1                   42           -.705         .942
  2                   43           -.364         .929
  3                   51            .213         .856
  4                   64            .537         .971

  VAR 5 VS.   VAR 2
  --------   -------
CATEGORY   NUMBER OF OBSERVATIONS   MEAN  STANDARD DEVIATION
--------   ----------------------   ----  ------------------
  1                   42           -.581         .826
  2                   43           -.338        1.069
  3                   51           -.009         .706
  4                   64            .615         .982

                  CORRELATIONS AND TEST STATISTICS
      (PE=PEARSON PRODUCT MOMENT, PC=POLYCHORIC, PS=POLYSERIAL)

                                 TEST OF MODEL         TEST OF ZERO CORR.
```

	CORRELATION	CHI-SQU.	DF	P-VALUE	CHI-SQU.	P-VALUE
VAR 2 VS. VAR 1	.471 (PE)				51.474	.000
VAR 3 VS. VAR 1	.497 (PS)	1.288	1	.256	58.488	.000
VAR 3 VS. VAR 2	.488 (PS)	1.255	1	.263	55.945	.000
VAR 4 VS. VAR 1	.476 (PS)	3.836	3	.280	52.722	.000
VAR 4 VS. VAR 2	.391 (PS)	1.201	3	.753	33.524	.000
VAR 4 VS. VAR 3	.544 (PC)	.409	1	.522	73.247	.000
VAR 5 VS. VAR 1	.495 (PS)	2.581	5	.764	57.996	.000
VAR 5 VS. VAR 2	.485 (PS)	11.047	5	.050	55.286	.000
VAR 5 VS. VAR 3	.531 (PC)	3.661	2	.160	68.918	.000
VAR 5 VS. VAR 4	.532 (PC)	7.096	5	.214	69.373	.000

ESTIMATED CORRELATION MATRIX

	VAR 1	VAR 2	VAR 3	VAR 4	VAR 5
VAR 1	1.000				
VAR 2	.471	1.000			
VAR 3	.497	.488	1.000		
VAR 4	.476	.391	.544	1.000	
VAR 5	.495	.485	.531	.532	1.000

All polychoric and polyserial correlations are closer to the true value 0.5 than were the corresponding product-moment correlations in Example 5B.

ASYMPTOTIC COVARIANCE MATRIX OF ESTIMATED CORRELATIONS

	R(2,1)	R(3,1)	R(3,2)	R(4,1)	R(4,2)	R(4,3)
R(2,1)	.00342					
R(3,1)	-.00111	.01333				
R(3,2)	-.00111	.00314	.01300			
R(4,1)	-.00096	.00346	.00100	.00921		
R(4,2)	-.00087	.00087	.00292	.00124	.00838	
R(4,3)	.00001	.00003	.00004	.00029	.00025	.00593
R(5,1)	-.00097	.00330	.00085	.00276	.00062	.00003
R(5,2)	-.00098	.00086	.00309	.00071	.00235	.00004
R(5,3)	-.00000	.00007	.00007	.00005	.00005	.00002
R(5,4)	.00001	.00003	.00003	.00028	.00024	.00019

ASYMPTOTIC COVARIANCE MATRIX OF ESTIMATED CORRELATIONS

	R(5,1)	R(5,2)	R(5,3)	R(5,4)
R(5,1)	.00879			
R(5,2)	.00142	.00858		
R(5,3)	.00043	.00042	.00564	
R(5,4)	.00040	.00040	.00024	.00426

The product-moment correlation R(2,1) has a smaller variance than the polychoric correlations R(4,3), R(5,3), and R(5,4), which in turn have smaller variances than the polyserial correlations. Note that the variances of the polychoric and polyserial correlations tend to get smaller as the number of categories increases.

A LISREL Example

In this section we illustrate the processes of (a) writing input for LISREL 7 and (b) interpreting the output from the program. The example presented is the hypothetical model discussed in *LISREL 7: A Guide to the Program and Applications* (the path diagram for this model is contained in Figure 1.1 of that textbook). This model is typical of the structural equation models often tested by researchers. It demonstrates many traditional features of LISREL. Further examples involving multiple groups, mean structures, use of equality constraints or non-normal variables can be found in *LISREL 7: A Guide to the Program and Applications.*

For most models, the LISREL subcommands perform the following tasks:

1. Specify characteristics of the data set, such as the number of variables, the names of the variables, and the form of the data (raw data, or summary statistics such as variances and covariances). If the data source is an SPSS active system file, most of this is done automatically.

2. Specify the general characteristics of the model: how many latent and observed exogenous and endogenous variables are there; what will be the form of each matrix in the model (for example, if square, is it symmetric or diagonal?); will each matrix consist primarily of free or of fixed parameters?

3. Specify modifications to individual elements of matrices to make them fixed in a predominantly free matrix, or vice versa; or specify sets of parameters to be equal.

4. Assign values to nonzero fixed parameters, and any other values necessary to start the iteration procedure.

5. Specify what output is desired, and nondefault settings to determine characteristics of the estimation process or output.

The Command File for testing this model is listed below, followed by a detailed explanation of each line.

```
TITLE "Demonstration of LISREL 7 within SPSS"
MATRIX DATA VARIABLES=Y_1 TO Y_4 X_1 TO X_7 / CONTENTS N COV
BEGIN DATA
  100   100   100   100   100   100   100   100   100   100   100
3.204
2.722 2.629
3.198 2.875 4.855
3.545 3.202 5.373 6.315
 .329  .371 -.357 -.471 1.363
```

```
 .559  .592 -.316 -.335 1.271 1.960
1.006 1.019 -.489 -.591 1.742 2.276 3.803
 .468  .456 -.438 -.539  .788 1.043 1.953 1.376
 .502  .539 -.363 -.425  .838 1.070 2.090 1.189 1.741
1.050  .960 1.416 1.714  .474  .694  .655  .071  .104 1.422
1.260 1.154 1.923 2.309  .686  .907  .917  .136  .162 1.688
2.684
END DATA
LISREL
 /"HYPOTHETICAL MODEL ESTIMATED BY ML"
 /DA NI=11
 /MO NY=4 NX=7 NE=2 NK=3 BE=FU
 /FR LY 2 1 LY 4 2 LX 2 1 LX 3 1 LX 3 2 LX 5 2 LX 7 3 BE 2 1 BE 1 2
 /FI GA 1 3 GA 2 2
 /VA 1 LY 1 1 LY 3 2 LX 1 1 LX 4 2 LX 6 3
 /LE
 /ETA_1 ETA_2
 /LK
 /KSI_1 KSI_2 KSI_3
 /OU SE TV MI RS EF MR SS TO
FINISH
```

First an active SPSS matrix system file is created containing the covariance matrix to be analyzed, the names of the variables, and the number of cases for each variable. The format of the matrix is subdiagonal (including the diagonal), which is the default. LISREL will use this matrix, because none of the LISREL subcommands specifies another input source. With the subcommand `MATRIX IN (*)` LISREL would have been told explicitly to use this matrix; the star (*) indicates the active file.

The order of the variables in the matrix is also the order we want in the LISREL analysis; that is, first the y-variables, then the x-variables. Therefore, the LISREL `SE` subcommand, which allows selection and reordering of the variables, is not used.

The first LISREL subcommand is a title. The title can extend for as many lines as needed (see the example in the LISREL Subcommand Reference); the program assumes that the title ends when it finds the characters "DA" as the first two characters of a subcommand, which signals the DAta subcommand.

The next subcommand is the DAta line. The keyword NI indicates the number of variables, which for this problem is 11. The keyword NO, for the number of cases (or observations) is not required, since it will be passed from the matrix system file. Other defaults not given on this subcommand are `NG=1` for a single group analysis, and `MA=CM`, indicating that a covariance matrix will be analyzed.

The MOdel parameters subcommand is used to specify the general form of the matrices in the model. There are four y-variables (NY=4), seven x-variables (NX=7), two η-variables (NE=2), and three ξ-variables (NK=3). The default form is used for most of the matrices; for example, $\mathbf{\Lambda}_x$ and $\mathbf{\Lambda}_y$ are FUll (i.e., rectangular, not square) matrices with FIxed elements. The only nondefault matrix form specified is BE=FU, which makes BEta a FUll rectangular matrix instead of the default, a ZEro matrix.

The specifications for individual elements that will depart from the general form specified in the MO subcommand are given next. The FRee subcommand allows parameters in matrices that were fixed to be free. The elements to be freed are specified by two-character names and indices to specify the row and column. For example, the first element freed is LY 2 1, which is the element in row 2, column 1, of Λ_y. The FI subcommand serves a similar purpose: it fixes elements in matrices that were specified to be free.

The VA subcommand gives specified values to parameters. If these parameters are fixed, then the values do not change during the estimation process. If no value is specified for a fixed parameter, its value defaults to zero. Here, the value 1 is given to various elements of Λ_y and Λ_x to define the scales of the five latent variables in the model.

The LE subcommand gives labels to the η-variables, and the LK subcommand gives labels to the ξ-variables. In the example, we have given generic names to these variables. Note that a delimiting slash is required before the names are listed. LISREL allows blanks within the variable names, but this requires a protection with single quotes. However, before LISREL sees the Command File, SPSS screens it and it would strip those apostrophes. Thus, `"'VAR 1'"` would be needed to preserve that blank. Several examples in *LISREL 7: A Guide to the Program and Applications* use hyphens within variable names, like ETA-1, a practice that the SPSS language does not allow. Single quotes would solve this problem: `'ETA-1'`.

The OU subcommand serves several purposes. Most commonly, it is used to specify the method of estimation (here maximum likelihood by default, since no other method is specified), and to specify what output is desired. Here we have requested the printing of standard errors (SE), t-values (TV), modification indices (MI), and the fitted covariance matrix, residuals, standardized residuals, and a Q-plot of residuals (RS), total and indirect effects (EF), miscellaneous results (MR) and a standardized solution (SS). The TO option requests that the output will be produced in 80-column format; the default on mainframe computers is 132 columns.

The (edited) output follows. Some segments are omitted to save space. Comments are interspersed, and are set off in italics to differentiate them from the actual output.

The program first reproduces the Command File. Note that several LISREL subcommands have been adjusted by the SPSS interface. For instance, the NO *keyword on the DA subcommand has been set.*

```
THE FOLLOWING LISREL CONTROL LINES HAVE BEEN READ :

 HYPOTHETICAL MODEL ESTIMATED BY ML
 DA NI=11  NO=  0.100000E+03
 CM FI=LSLDD21 FO
 (5E14.6)
  . . .
  . . .
  . . .
 OU SE TV MI RS EF MR SS
```

The program next displays the general form of the problem.

```
 HYPOTHETICAL MODEL ESTIMATED BY ML

                                  NUMBER OF INPUT VARIABLES 11
                                  NUMBER OF Y - VARIABLES    4
                                  NUMBER OF X - VARIABLES    7
                                  NUMBER OF ETA - VARIABLES  2
                                  NUMBER OF KSI - VARIABLES  3
                                  NUMBER OF OBSERVATIONS   100
```

The covariance matrix is listed. In some cases, this is calculated by the program from raw data, or from correlations and standard deviations.

```
          COVARIANCE MATRIX TO BE ANALYZED
```

	Y_1	Y_2	Y_3	Y_4	X_1	X_2
Y_1	3.204					
Y_2	2.722	2.629				
Y_3	3.198	2.875	4.855			
Y_4	3.545	3.202	5.373	6.315		
X_1	.329	.371	-.357	-.471	1.363	
X_2	.559	.592	-.316	-.335	1.271	1.960
X_3	1.006	1.019	-.489	-.591	1.742	2.276
X_4	.468	.456	-.438	-.539	.788	1.043
X_5	.502	.539	-.363	-.425	.838	1.070
X_6	1.050	.960	1.416	1.714	.474	.694
X_7	1.260	1.154	1.923	2.309	.686	.907

	X_3	X_4	X_5	X_6	X_7
X_3	3.803				
X_4	1.953	1.376			
X_5	2.090	1.189	1.741		
X_6	.655	.071	.104	1.422	
X_7	.917	.136	.162	1.688	2.684

For each matrix, the free and fixed elements are listed. Each parameter is assigned a number. The number zero indicates that an element is fixed; a positive integer that an element is free. When there are equality constraints, elements restricted to have the same value are assigned the same number. The specifications are a result of the general forms for the matrices that were specified in the MO subcommand, and the specifications for individual parameters in FI and FR subcommands.

PARAMETER SPECIFICATIONS

Lambda-Y has only two free parameters, which were specified on the FR line in the input. Remember that the value "0" for the other six parameters merely indicates that they are fixed, NOT that they are fixed at the value 0. In fact, two of them are fixed at the value 1, as can be seen in both the initial and final parameter estimates.

LAMBDA Y

	ETA_1	ETA_2
Y_1	0	0
Y_2	1	0
Y_3	0	0
Y_4	0	2

LAMBDA X

	KSI_1	KSI_2	KSI_3
X_1	0	0	0
X_2	3	0	0
X_3	4	5	0
X_4	0	0	0
X_5	0	6	0
X_6	0	0	0
X_7	0	0	7

BETA

	ETA_1	ETA_2
ETA_1	0	8
ETA_2	9	0

GAMMA

	KSI_1	KSI_2	KSI_3
ETA_1	10	11	0
ETA_2	12	0	13

For symmetric matrices such as PHI and PSI below, only the lower triangular part is specified.

PHI

	KSI_1	KSI_2	KSI_3
KSI_1	14		
KSI_2	15	16	
KSI_3	17	18	19

PSI

	ETA_1	ETA_2
ETA_1	20	
ETA_2	21	22

For diagonal matrices such as THETA EPS and THETA DELTA, only the diagonal elements are listed. Each of these matrices is actually a square matrix.

THETA EPS

Y_1	Y_2	Y_3	Y_4
23	24	25	26

THETA DELTA

X_1	X_2	X_3	X_4	X_5	X_6
27	28	29	30	31	32

X_7
33

Since the free parameters are numbered consecutively, it is easy to calculate the degrees of freedom: there are $(11 \times 12)/2 = 66$ *variances and covariances, and 33 free parameters, resulting in* $66 - 33 = 33$ *degrees of freedom.*

Next the initial estimates are reported. These were produced by two-stage least squares. They will often be close to the final values produced by maximum likelihood estimation.

INITIAL ESTIMATES (TSLS)

LAMBDA Y

	ETA_1	ETA_2
Y_1	1.000	.000
Y_2	.920	.000
Y_3	.000	1.000
Y_4	.000	1.135

LAMBDA X

	KSI_1	KSI_2	KSI_3
X_1	1.000	.000	.000
X_2	1.256	.000	.000
X_3	.826	1.143	.000
X_4	.000	1.000	.000
X_5	.000	1.076	.000
X_6	.000	.000	1.000
X_7	.000	.000	1.388

THETA DELTA

X_1	X_2	X_3	X_4	X_5	X_6
.334	.338	.118	.260	.450	.206

X_7
.340

Some additional output related to these initial estimates has been omitted here.

Now the maximum likelihood estimates are printed.

LISREL ESTIMATES (MAXIMUM LIKELIHOOD)

LAMBDA Y

	ETA_1	ETA_2
Y_1	1.000	.000
Y_2	.921	.000
Y_3	.000	1.000
Y_4	.000	1.139

LAMBDA X

	KSI_1	KSI_2	KSI_3
X_1	1.000	.000	.000
X_2	1.291	.000	.000
X_3	.920	1.092	.000
X_4	.000	1.000	.000
X_5	.000	1.079	.000
X_6	.000	.000	1.000
X_7	.000	.000	1.437

BETA

	ETA_1	ETA_2
ETA_1	.000	.538
ETA_2	.937	.000

GAMMA

	KSI_1	KSI_2	KSI_3
ETA_1	.213	.495	.000
ETA_2	-1.223	.000	.996

The variances and covariances among the ksi's, in the lower right-hand part of the following matrix, are the elements of the parameter matrix phi. The remaining elements are not part of the parameter estimates, but are derived from them.

COVARIANCE MATRIX OF ETA AND KSI

	ETA_1	ETA_2	KSI_1	KSI_2	KSI_3
ETA_1	2.957				
ETA_2	3.115	4.719			
KSI_1	.482	-.217	.974		
KSI_2	.554	-.312	.788	1.117	
KSI_3	.932	1.402	.525	.133	1.175

PSI

	ETA_1	ETA_2
ETA_1	.486	
ETA_2	-.069	.133

THETA EPS

Y_1	Y_2	Y_3	Y_4
.247	.123	.136	.197

THETA DELTA

X_1	X_2	X_3	X_4	X_5	X_6
.389	.336	.063	.259	.440	.247

X_7
.259

Now some other estimates that are derived from the parameter estimates are printed. These will help determine how well the observed variables measure the constructs, both individually and as a group. Here, the multiple correlations for the observed variables are all high, so none is a poor measure of its latent variable. The squared multiple correlations for the structural equations indicate the proportion of variance in the endogenous variables accounted for by the variables in the structural equations. Here they are very high.

SQUARED MULTIPLE CORRELATIONS FOR Y - VARIABLES

Y_1	Y_2	Y_3	Y_4
.923	.953	.972	.969

TOTAL COEFFICIENT OF DETERMINATION FOR Y - VARIABLES IS .999

SQUARED MULTIPLE CORRELATIONS FOR X - VARIABLES

X_1	X_2	X_3	X_4	X_5	X_6
.715	.829	.983	.812	.747	.826

X_7
.903

TOTAL COEFFICIENT OF DETERMINATION FOR X - VARIABLES IS 1.000

SQUARED MULTIPLE CORRELATIONS FOR STRUCTURAL EQUATIONS

ETA_1	ETA_2
.836	.972

TOTAL COEFFICIENT OF DETERMINATION FOR STRUCTURAL EQUATIONS IS .986

Some measures of fit of the model follow.

```
CHI-SQUARE WITH  33 DEGREES OF FREEDOM =    29.10 (P = .662)
                  GOODNESS OF FIT INDEX =  .953
         ADJUSTED GOODNESS OF FIT INDEX =  .906
             ROOT MEAN SQUARE RESIDUAL =  .065
```

The residuals compare the observed variances and covariances with those resulting from the model's parameter estimates. In a model that fits well, these will be small. The square root of the average squared residual was reported above as .065; the following table shows where the large residuals were, and how many there were. When examining these, keep in mind that their size will vary with the scale of the variables; changing the unit of measurement of a variable will change the variances and covariances, and thus the size of the residuals. Thus, caution is needed in the interpretation of these residuals.

FITTED COVARIANCE MATRIX

	Y_1	Y_2	Y_3	Y_4	X_1	X_2
Y_1	3.204					
Y_2	2.722	2.629				
Y_3	3.115	2.868	4.855			
Y_4	3.547	3.266	5.373	6.315		
X_1	.482	.444	-.217	-.247	1.363	
X_2	.622	.573	-.280	-.318	1.258	1.960
X_3	1.048	.965	-.540	-.614	1.757	2.269
X_4	.554	.510	-.312	-.355	.788	1.018
X_5	.598	.550	-.336	-.383	.851	1.098
X_6	.932	.858	1.402	1.596	.525	.678
X_7	1.339	1.233	2.014	2.293	.754	.974

	X_3	X_4	X_5	X_6	X_7
X_3	3.803				
X_4	1.945	1.376			
X_5	2.099	1.206	1.741		
X_6	.629	.133	.144	1.422	
X_7	.903	.192	.207	1.688	2.684

FITTED RESIDUALS

	Y_1	Y_2	Y_3	Y_4	X_1	X_2
Y_1	.000					
Y_2	.000	.000				
Y_3	.083	.007	.000			
Y_4	-.002	-.064	.000	.000		
X_1	-.153	-.073	-.140	-.224	.000	
X_2	-.063	.019	-.036	-.017	.013	.000
X_3	-.042	.054	.051	.023	-.015	.007
X_4	-.086	-.054	-.126	-.184	-.000	.025
X_5	-.096	-.011	-.027	-.042	-.013	-.028
X_6	.118	.102	.014	.118	-.051	.016
X_7	-.079	-.079	-.091	.016	-.068	-.067

	X_3	X_4	X_5	X_6	X_7
X_3	.000				
X_4	.008	.000			
X_5	-.009	-.017	.000		
X_6	.026	-.062	-.040	.000	
X_7	.014	-.056	-.045	.000	.000

SUMMARY STATISTICS FOR FITTED RESIDUALS

```
SMALLEST FITTED RESIDUAL =    -.224
  MEDIAN FITTED RESIDUAL =    -.001
 LARGEST FITTED RESIDUAL =     .118
```

The stem-and-leaf plot is useful for detecting residuals that are outliers, and for examining the general shape of the distribution of residuals.

STEMLEAF PLOT

```
- 2–2
- 1–85
- 1–430
- 0–9988777666655
- 0–44444332211110000000000000000
  0–111111222233
  0–558
  1–022
```

The standardized residuals are the residuals divided by their standard errors.

STANDARDIZED RESIDUALS

	Y_1	Y_2	Y_3	Y_4	X_1	X_2
Y_1	.000					
Y_2	.000	.000				
Y_3	1.661	.215	.000			
Y_4	-.040	-1.665	.000	.000		
X_1	-1.500	-.829	-1.143	-1.592	.000	
X_2	-.708	.266	-.364	-.144	.584	.000
X_3	-.560	1.269	.929	.346	-.451	.349
X_4	-1.023	-.773	-1.290	-1.633	-.002	.596
X_5	-.863	-.119	-.199	-.274	-.203	-.485
X_6	1.641	1.743	.201	1.447	-.761	.256
X_7	-1.112	-1.576	-1.546	.229	-.839	-1.006

	X_3	X_4	X_5	X_6	X_7
X_3	.000				
X_4	.530	.000			
X_5	-.372	-1.077	.000		
X_6	.351	-.982	-.490	.000	
X_7	.249	-.794	-.462	.000	.000

The summary statistics, stem-and-leaf display, and list of outlying standardized residuals below make it much easier than examining the above display to see how bad the fit is. But the display of all the standardized residuals may help locate the reasons why a model does not fit well.

SUMMARY STATISTICS FOR STANDARDIZED RESIDUALS

```
SMALLEST STANDARDIZED RESIDUAL =   -1.665
  MEDIAN STANDARDIZED RESIDUAL =    -.023
 LARGEST STANDARDIZED RESIDUAL =    1.743
```

QPLOT OF STANDARDIZED RESIDUALS

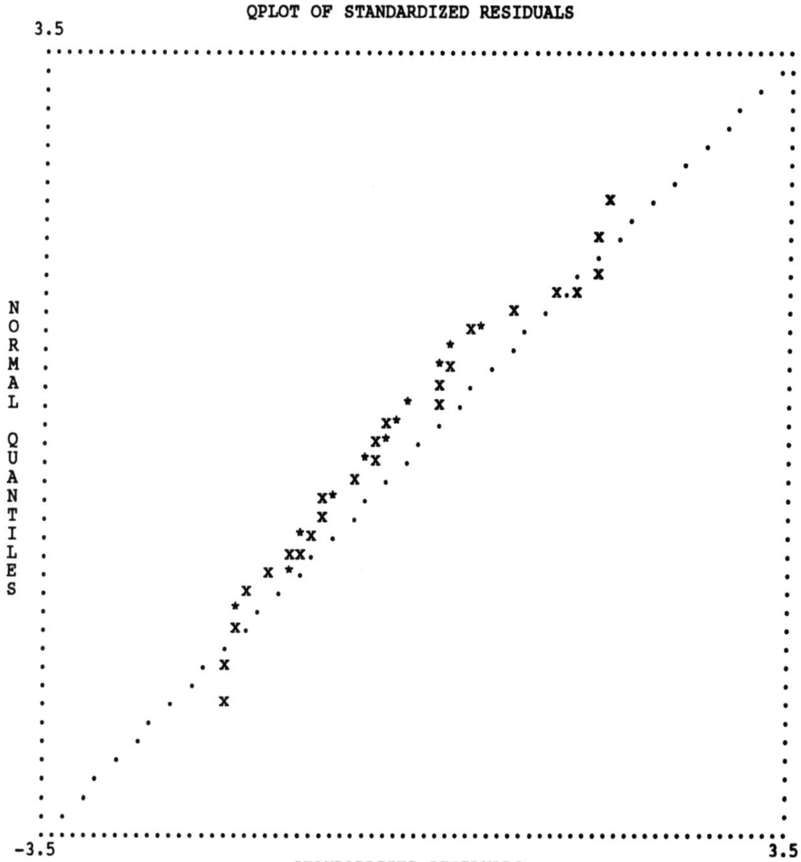

```
STEMLEAF PLOT

 - 1–766655
 - 1–3111000
 - 0–988888765555
 - 0–44322110000000000000000
   0–222233334
   0–5669
   1–34
   1–677
```

The plot above is another way of examining standardized residuals. For a poorly fitting model the plot will be shallower than the diagonal line. If the standardized residuals are very small, then the plot will be steeper than the diagonal line. An x *represents a single point, an* $*$ *multiple points. Nonlinearities in the plotted points are indicative of specification errors in the model or of departures from linearity or normality.*

The standard errors below show how accurately the values of the free parameters have been estimated. If these are small, as they mostly are here, then the parameters have been estimated accurately.

STANDARD ERRORS

LAMBDA Y

	ETA_1	ETA_2
Y_1	.000	.000
Y_2	.035	.000
Y_3	.000	.000
Y_4	.000	.029

LAMBDA X

	KSI_1	KSI_2	KSI_3
X_1	.000	.000	.000
X_2	.105	.000	.000
X_3	.123	.117	.000
X_4	.000	.000	.000
X_5	.000	.084	.000
X_6	.000	.000	.000
X_7	.000	.000	.093

BETA

	ETA_1	ETA_2
ETA_1	.000	.056
ETA_2	.178	.000

GAMMA

	KSI_1	KSI_2	KSI_3
ETA_1	.154	.148	.000
ETA_2	.122	.000	.152

PHI

	KSI_1	KSI_2	KSI_3
KSI_1	.188		
KSI_2	.151	.195	
KSI_3	.134	.126	.203

PSI

	ETA_1	ETA_2
ETA_1	.127	
ETA_2	.169	.078

THETA EPS

Y_1	Y_2	Y_3	Y_4
.053	.038	.041	.055

THETA DELTA

X_1	X_2	X_3	X_4	X_5	X_6
.064	.067	.051	.050	.075	.054

X_7
.092

For each free parameter, the parameter estimate divided by its standard error produces a t-value. If a t-value is between -1.96 *and* 1.96*, it is not significantly different from zero, so fixing it to zero will not make the fit of the model significantly worse.*

As an example, to test whether the covariance between KSI2 and KSI3 is zero, we examine the t-value .133/.126 = 1.056. So this covariance is not significantly different from zero.

T-VALUES

LAMBDA Y

	ETA_1	ETA_2
Y_1	.000	.000
Y_2	25.993	.000
Y_3	.000	.000
Y_4	.000	38.739

LAMBDA X

	KSI_1	KSI_2	KSI_3
X_1	.000	.000	.000
X_2	12.335	.000	.000
X_3	7.462	9.318	.000
X_4	.000	.000	.000
X_5	.000	12.798	.000
X_6	.000	.000	.000
X_7	.000	.000	15.479

BETA

	ETA_1	ETA_2
ETA_1	.000	9.525
ETA_2	5.255	.000

GAMMA

	KSI_1	KSI_2	KSI_3
ETA_1	1.389	3.351	.000
ETA_2	-10.052	.000	6.566

PHI

	KSI_1	KSI_2	KSI_3
KSI_1	5.170		
KSI_2	5.212	5.725	
KSI_3	3.927	1.059	5.784

PSI

	ETA_1	ETA_2
ETA_1	3.834	
ETA_2	-.408	1.698

THETA EPS

Y_1	Y_2	Y_3	Y_4
4.663	3.240	3.325	3.603

THETA DELTA

X_1	X_2	X_3	X_4	X_5	X_6
6.094	5.001	1.229	5.136	5.875	4.596

X_7
2.827

The effects of one variable on another can be direct, most of which are seen in a path diagram as one-way arrows; they are parameters in the model. Others are found by computing the reduced form equations (see LISREL 7: A Guide to the Program and Applications). The total effects include the direct effects, as well as indirect effects that result from correlations among exogenous variables and circular or reciprocal effects.

TOTAL AND INDIRECT EFFECTS

TOTAL EFFECTS OF KSI ON ETA

	KSI_1	KSI_2	KSI_3
ETA_1	-.895	.999	1.080
ETA_2	-2.062	.936	2.008

The standard errors can be used to test whether the effects differ significantly from zero.

STANDARD ERRORS FOR TOTAL EFFECTS OF KSI ON ETA

	KSI_1	KSI_2	KSI_3
ETA_1	.428	.342	.224
ETA_2	.517	.403	.268

INDIRECT EFFECTS OF KSI ON ETA

	KSI_1	KSI_2	KSI_3
ETA_1	-1.109	.503	1.080
ETA_2	-.839	.936	1.012

STANDARD ERRORS FOR INDIRECT EFFECTS OF KSI ON ETA

	KSI_1	KSI_2	KSI_3
ETA_1	.340	.240	.224
ETA_2	.466	.403	.309

TOTAL EFFECTS OF ETA ON ETA

	ETA_1	ETA_2
ETA_1	1.016	1.084
ETA_2	1.890	1.016

The stability index is used in models with reciprocal or circular paths. As long as it is less than 1, there is no problem: the system is stable, and the total effects are finite.

LARGEST EIGENVALUE OF B*B' (STABILITY INDEX) IS .879

STANDARD ERRORS FOR TOTAL EFFECTS OF ETA ON ETA

	ETA_1	ETA_2
ETA_1	.410	.282
ETA_2	.717	.410

INDIRECT EFFECTS OF ETA ON ETA

	ETA_1	ETA_2
ETA_1	1.016	.546
ETA_2	.953	1.016

STANDARD ERRORS FOR INDIRECT EFFECTS OF ETA ON ETA

	ETA_1	ETA_2
ETA_1	.410	.247
ETA_2	.548	.410

TOTAL EFFECTS OF ETA ON Y

	ETA_1	ETA_2
Y_1	2.016	1.084
Y_2	1.856	.998
Y_3	1.890	2.016
Y_4	2.152	2.296

STANDARD ERRORS FOR TOTAL EFFECTS OF ETA ON Y

	ETA_1	ETA_2
Y_1	.410	.282
Y_2	.384	.259
Y_3	.717	.410
Y_4	.817	.471

INDIRECT EFFECTS OF ETA ON Y

	ETA_1	ETA_2
Y_1	1.016	1.084
Y_2	.936	.998
Y_3	1.890	1.016
Y_4	2.152	1.157

STANDARD ERRORS FOR INDIRECT EFFECTS OF ETA ON Y

	ETA_1	ETA_2
Y_1	.410	.282
Y_2	.380	.259
Y_3	.717	.410
Y_4	.817	.468

TOTAL EFFECTS OF KSI ON Y

	KSI_1	KSI_2	KSI_3
Y_1	-.895	.999	1.080
Y_2	-.824	.919	.994
Y_3	-2.062	.936	2.008
Y_4	-2.348	1.066	2.287

STANDARD ERRORS FOR TOTAL EFFECTS OF KSI ON Y

	KSI_1	KSI_2	KSI_3
Y_1	.428	.342	.224
Y_2	.394	.315	.206
Y_3	.517	.403	.268
Y_4	.589	.459	.306

Next are the variances and covariances that are not parameters of the model, but are derived from them. These are produced by the MR option on the OU line.

COVARIANCES

Y - ETA

	Y_1	Y_2	Y_3	Y_4
ETA_1	2.957	2.722	3.115	3.547
ETA_2	3.115	2.868	4.719	5.373

Y - KSI

	Y_1	Y_2	Y_3	Y_4
KSI_1	.482	.444	-.217	-.247
KSI_2	.554	.510	-.312	-.355
KSI_3	.932	.858	1.402	1.596

X - ETA

	X_1	X_2	X_3	X_4	X_5	X_6
ETA_1	.482	.622	1.048	.554	.598	.932
ETA_2	-.217	-.280	-.540	-.312	-.336	1.402

	X_7
ETA_1	1.339
ETA_2	2.014

X - KSI

	X_1	X_2	X_3	X_4	X_5	X_6
KSI_1	.974	1.258	1.757	.788	.851	.525
KSI_2	.788	1.018	1.945	1.117	1.206	.133
KSI_3	.525	.678	.629	.133	.144	1.175

	X_7
KSI_1	.754
KSI_2	.192
KSI_3	1.688

In the standardized solution, all latent variables are standardized, i.e., they have a mean of zero and a standard deviation of one.

STANDARDIZED SOLUTION

LAMBDA Y

	ETA_1	ETA_2
Y_1	1.719	.000
Y_2	1.583	.000
Y_3	.000	2.172
Y_4	.000	2.474

LAMBDA X

	KSI_1	KSI_2	KSI_3
X_1	.987	.000	.000
X_2	1.274	.000	.000
X_3	.908	1.154	.000
X_4	.000	1.057	.000
X_5	.000	1.141	.000
X_6	.000	.000	1.084
X_7	.000	.000	1.557

BETA

	ETA_1	ETA_2
ETA_1	.000	.679
ETA_2	.742	.000

GAMMA

	KSI_1	KSI_2	KSI_3
ETA_1	.123	.304	.000
ETA_2	-.556	.000	.497

The correlations among the latent variables presented below are often much easier to interpret than the variances and covariances calculated above.

CORRELATION MATRIX OF ETA AND KSI

	ETA_1	ETA_2	KSI_1	KSI_2	KSI_3
ETA_1	1.000				
ETA_2	.834	1.000			
KSI_1	.284	-.101	1.000		
KSI_2	.305	-.136	.756	1.000	
KSI_3	.500	.595	.491	.117	1.000

PSI

	ETA_1	ETA_2
ETA_1	.164	
ETA_2	-.018	.028

REGRESSION MATRIX ETA ON KSI (STANDARDIZED)

	KSI_1	KSI_2	KSI_3
ETA_1	-.514	.614	.681
ETA_2	-.937	.455	1.002

When a model does not fit well, the modification indices will often be the most useful way of deciding how to change the model to improve the fit. They give an estimate of how much the chi-square will decrease if a fixed parameter is freed. Of course, a parameter should only be freed if it makes sense to do so. The estimated change shows approximately how much the parameter will change when it is freed.

MODIFICATION INDICES AND ESTIMATED CHANGE

MODIFICATION INDICES FOR LAMBDA Y

	ETA_1	ETA_2
Y_1	.000	.990
Y_2	.000	.990
Y_3	2.115	.000
Y_4	2.115	.000

ESTIMATED CHANGE FOR LAMBDA Y

	ETA_1	ETA_2
Y_1	.000	.058
Y_2	.000	-.053
Y_3	.089	.000
Y_4	-.102	.000

MODIFICATION INDICES FOR LAMBDA X

	KSI_1	KSI_2	KSI_3
X_1	.000	.108	1.049
X_2	.000	.108	.342
X_3	.000	.000	3.376
X_4	.304	.000	1.373
X_5	.304	.000	.241
X_6	.208	.001	.000
X_7	.208	.001	.000

ESTIMATED CHANGE FOR LAMBDA X

	KSI_1	KSI_2	KSI_3
X_1	.000	-.044	-.082
X_2	.000	.057	-.054
X_3	.000	.000	.148
X_4	.082	.000	-.077
X_5	-.089	.000	-.038
X_6	.034	-.001	.000
X_7	-.048	.002	.000

```
NO NON-ZERO MODIFICATION INDICES FOR BETA
NO NON-ZERO MODIFICATION INDICES FOR GAMMA
NO NON-ZERO MODIFICATION INDICES FOR PHI
NO NON-ZERO MODIFICATION INDICES FOR PSI
NO NON-ZERO MODIFICATION INDICES FOR THETA EPS
NO NON-ZERO MODIFICATION INDICES FOR THETA DELTA

      MAXIMUM MODIFICATION INDEX IS   3.38 FOR ELEMENT ( 3, 3) OF LAMBDA X
```

This analysis shows that the model fits the data well. In LISREL 7: A Guide to the Program and Applications, several examples illustrate what can be done when this is not the case. For instance, detecting misspecification of a model (Example 5.3), evaluating alternative models (Examples 5.6 and 6.4) and how to deal with a nonidentified model (Example 6.6). Example 8.1 illustrates that sometimes the data are to blame, which leads to nonadmissible solutions in that case. Finally, Chapter 11 gives some hints on what can be done when everything else fails.

References

References

Bock, R. D., and Lieberman, M. (1970). Fitting a response model for *n* dichotomously scored items. *Psychometrika*, **35**, 179–197.

Browne, M. W. (1974). Generalized least squares estimators in the analysis of covariance structures. *South African Statistical Journal*, **8**, 1–24. (Reprinted in D. J. Aigner and A. S. Goldberger (eds.), *Latent Variables in Socioeconomic Models*. Amsterdam: North Holland Publishing Co., 1977.)

Browne, M. W. (1982) Covariance structures. In D. M. Hawkins (ed.), *Topics in Applied Multivariate Analysis* (pp. 72–141). Cambridge: Cambridge University Press.

Browne, M. W. (1984). Asymptotically distribution-free methods for the analysis of covariance structures. *British Journal of Mathematical and Statistical Psychology*, **37**, 62–83.

Christoffersson, A. (1975). Factor analysis of dichotomized variables. *Psychometrika*, **40**, 5–32.

Finn, J. D. (1974). *A General Model for Multivariate Analysis*. New York: Holt, Reinhart, and Winston.

Guttman, L. A. (1953). Image theory for the structure of quantitative variates. *Psychometrika*, **18**, 277–296.

Hasselrot, T., and Lernberg, L. O. (eds.), (1980). *Tonåringen och Livet*. Vällingby, Sweden: Liber Forläg. (In Swedish)

Johnson, N. L., and Kotz, S. (1970). *Distributions in Statistics: Continuous Univariate Distributions-1*. New York: John Wiley & Sons.

Jöreskog, K. G. (1979). Basic ideas of factor and component analysis. Chapter 1 in K. G. Jöreskog and D. Sörbom (eds.), *Advances in Factor Analysis and Structural Equation Models*. Cambridge, MA: Abt Books.

Jöreskog, K. G. (1981). Analysis of covariance structures. *Scandinavian Journal of Statistics*, **8**, 65–92.

Jöreskog, K. G. (1986). Estimation of the polyserial correlation from summary statistics. Research Report 86–2. University of Uppsala, Department of Statistics.

Jöreskog, K. G., and Sörbom, D. (1988; 2nd edition). *PRELIS: A Preprocessor for LISREL*. Mooresville, IN: Scientific Software, Inc.

Jöreskog, K. G., and Sörbom, D. (1989). *LISREL 7: User's Reference Guide.* Mooresville, IN: Scientific Software, Inc.

Jöreskog, K. G., and Sörbom, D. (1989; 2nd edition). *LISREL 7: A Guide to the Program and Applications.* Chicago, IL: SPSS, Inc.

Kendall, M. G., and Stuart, A. (1961). *The Advanced Theory of Statistics, Vol. 2: Inference and Relationship.* London: Charles Griffin and Company, Ltd.

Kendall, M. G., and Stuart, A. (1963). *The Advanced Theory of Statistics, Vol. 1: Distribution Theory.* London: Charles Griffin and Company, Ltd.

Mardia, K. V. (1970). Measures of multivariate skewness and kurtosis with applications. *Biometrika*, **57**, 519–530.

Muthén, B. (1984). A general structural equation model with dichotomous, ordered categorical and continuous latent variable indicators. *Psychometrika*, **49**, 115–132.

Olsson, U. (1979). Maximum likelihood estimation of the polychoric correlation coefficient. *Psychometrika*, **44**, 443–460.

Tukey, J. W. (1977). *Exploratory Data Analysis.* Reading, MA: Addison-Wesley Publishing Company.

Appendixes

- *PRELIS Warnings and Error Messages*
- *LISREL Command Files*

Contents

PRELIS Warnings and Error Messages

The following warnings and error messages may be issued by the PRELIS program. The reason they are included in this appendix, as opposed to LISREL and SPSS warning and error messages, is the fact that they sometimes refer to native PRELIS syntax. As explained in Part A, this native syntax has been completely replaced by SPSS PRELIS syntax. Another consequence of this replacement is that some of those warnings and error messages are not applicable anymore, *i.e.*, they should not occur.

Here is an overview of all the warnings and error messages that are possible in native PRELIS.

- `SYNTAX ERROR` (codes 101 through 106)

  None of these syntax errors is applicable under SPSS PRELIS.

- `WARNING` (codes 201 through 219)

  Attention is called to a particular condition that does not immediately lead to a complete program stop, but may eventually lead to a fatal error. For example, a variance of 0, or a correlation of +1 or −1.

- `FATAL ERROR` (codes 301 through 309)

  Stop processing.

- `FATAL ERROR` (codes 401 through 408)

  None of these fatal errors should happen to the SPSS PRELIS user.

The following detailed list of applicable warnings and error messages has been ordered by the three-digit error code. Most messages are self-explanatory, but sometimes recommended solutions are provided.

201 `WARNING: xxxxxx has more than 15 categories and will be treated as continuous.`

The variable x, which is ordinal (either by your specification on the `VARIABLES` subcommand or because of the `MAXCAT` setting) has more than the maximum 15 distinct values, not counting missing values. If you are satisfied with treating this variable as continuous, nothing needs to be done. But if you really want to treat this variable as ordinal, you have to recode the variable into fewer categories.

202 `WARNING: Variable xxxxxx has no cases in category zz in the contingency table with variable yyyyyy. The column will be deleted in the computation of the polychoric correlation.`

The contingency table between the ordinal variables x and y has one empty column corresponding to category z of x. Although there are cases in category z in the univariate distribution of x, these cases have been eliminated in the bivariate distribution because all have missing values on variable y when pairwise deletion is used. The polychoric correlation can still be computed, provided there are at least two non-empty categories on both variables. If this is not the case, fatal error 306 will appear and processing will stop.

203 `WARNING: Variable xxxxxx has no cases in category zz in the contingency table with variable yyyyyy. The row will be deleted in the computation of the polychoric correlation.`

The contingency table between the ordinal variables x and y has one empty row corresponding to category z of x. Although there are cases in category z in the univariate distribution of x, these cases have been eliminated in the bivariate distribution because all have missing values on variable y when pairwise deletion is used. The polychoric correlation can still be computed provided there are at least two non-empty categories on both variables. If this is not the case, fatal error 306 will appear and processing will stop.

204 `WARNING: Category xx has been deleted in the computation of the polyserial correlation because of zero within variance.`

When this warning appears, the context will indicate the pair of variables for which polyserial correlation is being computed. Either there is only a single case in category x, or the values of the continuous variable corresponding to category x of the ordinal variable are all equal, and the variance of the continuous variable given category x of the ordinal variable is, therefore, zero. This category cannot be used in the computation of the polyserial correlation. (Recall that a polyserial correlation is a correlation between an ordinal and a continuous variable.) The polyserial correlation can still be computed, if there are at least two categories of the ordinal variable for which the within variance is positive. If this is not the case, fatal error 307 will appear.

205 `WARNING: The iterations did not converge. The correlation may not be correct.`

This warning should not occur. It means that the program has not been able to estimate a polychoric or polyserial correlation for a pair of variables. The context in which the warning appears will indicate the pair of variables and the type of correlation involved. The message is probably the result of a too-small (pairwise) sample and data that are inconsistent with assumptions underlying the polychoric and polyserial correlations.

206 `WARNING: The correlation is unity. Check your data.`

The estimated correlation for a pair of variables is 1. This may be unreasonable, so check your data. The pair of variables causing the problem will be clear from the context in which this message appears.

209 `WARNING: The asymptotic covariance matrix of estimated coefficients can only be estimated under listwise deletion.`

You have requested `WRITE=ACOV` with `MISSING PAIRWISE`. Change to `MISSING LISTWISE`.

210 `WARNING: The asymptotic covariance matrix of estimated coefficients is not available when MA=MM, MA=AM, or MA=OM.`

You have requested `TYPE = MOMENT`, `TYPE = AUGMENTED`, or `TYPE = OPTIMAL`.

211 `WARNING: The asymptotic variances of estimated coefficients can only be estimated under listwise deletion.`

You have requested `WRITE AVAR` with `MISSING = PAIRWISE`. Change to `MISSING LISTWISE`

212 `WARNING: The asymptotic variances of estimated coefficients is not available when MA=MM, MA=AM, or MA=OM.`

You have requested `TYPE = MOMENT`, `TYPE = AUGMENTED`, or `TYPE = OPTIMAL`.

215 `WARNING: Sample size too small. Asymptotic variances and covariances will not be computed.`

You have requested `WRITE ACOV` or `WRITE AVAR`, but your sample size is too small for these options. If you really need to compute asymptotic variances and/or covariances, you should add more cases. Or you can, at your own risk, change the program's sample size restriction. See the `CRITERIA` subcommand.

216 `WARNING: Error(s) occurred when computing asymptotic variances and covariances. Matrix not saved.`

The method for computing asymptotic variances and covariances requires that certain matrices be positive-definite. This error usually occurs when your sample is too small or your data are otherwise inadequate.

217 `WARNING: The Relative Multivariate Kurtosis measure is only available for TR=LI and MA=CM.`

You have requested `KURTOSIS` on the `PRINT` subcommand, but without specifying `MISSING LISTWISE` and `TYPE = COVARIANCE`.

218 **WARNING: The estimated covariance matrix is not positive-definite. The Relative Multivariate Kurtosis cannot be computed.**

There are two possible causes. Either one (or more) of your variables is a linear combination of other variables, or the sample size is smaller than the number of variables. Data of this kind are all right, but they cannot be used to compute Mardia's measure of relative multivariate kurtosis (which you have requested by specifying the KURTOSIS keyword on the PRINT subcommand.

219 **WARNING: xxxxxx has only one value.**

All cases have the same value on variable x (missing values excluded). If you have also specified TYPE = CORRELATION, TYPE = OPTIMAL, or TYPE = POLYCHOR, fatal error 304 will occur.

302 **FATAL ERROR: SAMPLE SIZE TOO SMALL FOR POLYCHORIC AND POLYSERIAL CORRELATIONS. PROBLEM NOT COMPLETED.**

Processing stops. You have requested TYPE = POLYCHOR either with a listwise sample size less than 20, or a pairwise sample size less than 20 for at least one pair of variables. Sample sizes less than 20 are really much too small to be able to estimate polychoric and/or polyserial correlations.

304 **FATAL ERROR: xxxxxx HAS ONLY ONE VALUE. PROBLEM NOT COMPLETED.**

Processing stops. The variable x has only one value, not counting missing values. The variance of this variable is, therefore, zero. The correlation matrix cannot be computed when this variable is included.

306 **FATAL ERROR: VARIABLE xxxxxx HAS LESS THAN TWO CATEGORIES FOR VARIABLE yyyyyy. POLYCHORIC CORRELATION CANNOT BE COMPUTED. PROBLEM NOT COMPLETED.**

Processing stops. The contingency table for variables x and y has only one row or only one column. This makes it impossible to estimate a polychoric correlation. This error may occur as a consequence of warnings 202 or 203.

307 **FATAL ERROR: ORDINAL VARIABLE xxxxxx HAS LESS THAN TWO CATEGORIES FOR VARIABLE yyyyyy. POLYSERIAL CORRELATION CANNOT BE COMPUTED. PROBLEM NOT COMPLETED.**

Processing stops. The polyserial correlation between variables x and y cannot be computed because ordinal variable x has only one category. This error may occur as a consequence of warning 204.

309 **FATAL ERROR: IMPOSSIBLE TO COMPUTE POLYSERIAL CORRELATION BETWEEN xxx AND yyy. PROBABLY SOMETHING IS WRONG IN YOUR DATA OR DATA FORMAT. PROBLEM NOT COMPLETED.**

Processing stops. This error should not occur. If it does, it is because something is wrong in your data.

LISREL Command Files

Following are some examples from the *"LISREL 7: A Guide to the Program and Applications"* textbook, adapted for use in SPSS LISREL. First, the last example from Chapter 5. A matrix system file with correlations and standard deviations is created. The command **MCONVERT** transforms it to a covariance matrix, which is then analyzed by LISREL.

```
MATRIX DATA VARIABLES=ROWTYPE_ PERFORMM JBSATIS1 JBSATIS2
                 ACHMOT1 ACHMOT2 T_S_S_E1 T_S_S_E2 VERBINTM
BEGIN DATA
'SD      '  2.09   3.43   2.81   1.95   2.06   2.16   2.06   3.65
'COR     ' 1.000
'COR     '  .418 1.000
'COR     '  .394   .627 1.000
'COR     '  .129   .202   .266 1.000
'COR     '  .189   .284   .208   .365 1.000
'COR     '  .544   .281   .324   .201   .161 1.000
'COR     '  .507   .225   .314   .172   .174   .546 1.000
'COR     ' -.357 -.156 -.038 -.199 -.277 -.294 -.174 1.000
END DATA
MCONVERT
LISREL
 /"EX 5.6: MODIFIED MODEL FOR PERFORMANCE AND SATISFACTION     "
 /"      REFERENCES                                             "
 /"BAGOZZI, R.P. PERFORMANCE AND SATISFACTION IN AN INDUSTRIAL"
 /"SALES FORCE. AN EXAMINATION OF THEIR ANTECEDENTS AND        "
 /"SIMULTANEITY.                                                "
 /"JOURNAL OF MARKETING 1980, 44, 65-77                         "
 /"                                                             "
 /"JORESKOG, K.G. AND SORBOM, D.                                "
 /"RECENT DEVELOPMENTS IN STRUCTURAL EQUATION MODELING.         "
 /"JOURNAL OF MARKETING RESEARCH, 1982, 19, 404-416.            "
 /"                                                             "
    /da ni=8 no=122
    /mo ny=3 nx=5 ne=2 nk=3 be=fu ps=di
    /le
    /perform jobsatis
    /lk                                /* NOTE QUOTES NEXT LINE
    /"achmot 't-s s-e' 'verb int'"
    /fr ly 3 2 lx 2 1 lx 4 2 be 2 1
    /fi te 1 td 5 ga 1 1 ga 2 2 ga 1 3
    /va 1 ly 1 1 ly 2 2 lx 1 1 lx 3 2 lx 5 3
    /va 1.998 td 5
    /ou se tv rs ef mi ss ad=off
FINISH
```

Next are some examples from Chapter 6. Note that in the second example the inline data that follow the **MA** subcommand are now given as the twelve separate rows of the Λ_x parameter matrix. They could have been given as just one long row (with 36 data), or in other forms. In the third example (6.4a–c) with data input from the active file, the complete data set is used automatically for each subcommand set.

```
TITLE "EXAMPLES FROM CHAPTER 6 IN LISREL 7 TEXTBOOK"
MATRIX DATA VARIABLES=VAR1 VAR2 VAR3 /FORMAT=FREE
    /CONTENTS COV /N=900
BEGIN DATA
54.85 60.21 99.24 48.42 67.00 63.81
END DATA
LISREL /MATRIX IN (*)
 /"EX 6.1: KRISTOF'S MODEL ESTIMATED FOR THREE SUBTESTS OF SAT"
    /DA NI=3 NG=1
    /MO NY=3 NE=3 NK=1 LY=DI,FR PH=ST PS=DI TE=ZE
    /EQ LY 1 GA 1 /EQ LY 2 GA 2 /EQ LY 3 GA 3 /EQ PS 1 - PS 3
    /ST 2 ALL
    /OU SE TV SO NS

MATRIX DATA VARIABLES=VAR1 TO VAR12 /CONTENTS=COV /N=107
BEGIN DATA
 51.6
-27.7  72.1
 38.9 -41.1  69.9
-36.4  40.7 -39.1  75.8
 13.8  -5.2  17.9   1.9  84.8
-13.6  10.9   9.5  17.8 -37.4  91.1
 21.5  -9.4   8.5 -13.1  59.7 -54.4  79.9
-12.8 -17.2  -3.1  22.0 -43.3  52.7 -49.9  87.2
 11.0  -8.9  19.2 -11.2 -12.6  21.9 -10.6  17.5  27.6
 -4.5  10.2  -7.6  12.7  20.4 -11.5  16.5 -14.8  -8.8  19.9
  9.2   -.3  18.9 -13.6  -3.9  19.0  -8.3  13.1  17.7  -2.8
 27.3
 -3.7   7.5  -4.5  12.8  19.9  -8.8  15.5  -8.6  -5.4  13.3
 -1.0  16.0
END DATA
LISREL
 /"EXAMPLE 6.3: THE ROD AND FRAME TEST        "
   /DA  NI = 12
   /MO  NX = 12  NK = 3  LX = FI  PH = DI
   /MA  LX
      /1   1   1    /1  -1  -1   /1   1   1    /1  -1  -1
      /1  -1   1    /1   1  -1   /1  -1   1    /1   1  -1
      /1   1   0    /1  -1   0   /1   1   0    /1  -1   0
   /EQ  TD(1)  TD(3) /EQ  TD(2)  TD(4)  /EQ  TD(5)  TD(7)
   /EQ  TD(6)  TD(8) /EQ  TD(9)  TD(11) /EQ  TD(10) TD(12)
   /OU  SE  TV

MATRIX DATA VARIABLES=
   ANOMIA67 POWER67 ANOMIA71 POWER71 EDUCATIN SOCIOIND
   /CONTENTS=COV /N=932
BEGIN DATA
 11.834
  6.947  9.364
```

```
  6.819   5.091 12.532
  4.783   5.028   7.495   9.986
 -3.839 -3.889 -3.841 -3.625  9.610
 -2.190 -1.883 -2.175 -1.878  3.552   4.503
END DATA
LISREL
 /"EXAMPLE 6.4A: STABILITY OF ALIENATION, MODEL A               "
 /"(UNCORRELATED ERROR TERM)                                    "
   / DA NI=6
   / SE / 1 2 3 4 /
   / MO NY=4 NE=2 BE=SD PS=DI TE=SY
   / LE / ALIEN67 ALIEN71
   /FR LY(2,1) LY(4,2)
   /VA 1 LY(1,1) LY(3,2)
   /OU SE TV MI ND=2
 /"EXAMPLE 6.4B: STABILITY OF ALIENATION, MODEL B"
   /DA NI=6 /MO NY=4 NX=2 NE=2 NK=1 BE=SD PS=DI TE=SY
   /LE /ALIEN67 ALIEN71
   /LK /SES
   /FR LY(2,1) LY(4,2) LX(2,1)
   /VA 1 LY(1,1) LY(3,2) LX(1,1)
   /OU SE TV MI ND=2
 /"EXAMPLE 6.4C: STABILITY OF ALIENATION, MODEL C"
 /" (CORRELATED ERRORS FOR ANOMIA67 AND ANOMIA71)"
   /DA NI=6
   /MO NY=4 NX=2 NE=2 NK=1 BE=SD PS=DI TE=SY
   /LE /ALIEN67 ALIEN71
   /LK /SES
   /FR LY(2,1) LY(4,2) LX(2,1) TE(3,1)
   /VA 1 LY(1,1) LY(3,2) LX(1,1)
   /OU SE TV MI ND=2 EF MR
FINISH
```

Finally, an example from Chapter 9, multi-sample analysis. A split-file is used, with the number of subcommand sets matching three split groups.

```
TITLE "USING SPLIT SYSTEM MATRIX FILE WITH MULTIGROUP PROBLEMS"
MATRIX DATA VARIABLES=SOFED SOMED SOFOC FAFED MOMED FAFOC
            /CONTENTS=COV N /SPLIT=SPL
BEGIN DATA
  5.86
  3.12   3.32
 35.28  23.85 622.09
  4.02   2.14  29.42   5.33
  2.99   2.55  19.20   3.17   4.64
 35.30  26.91 465.62  31.22  23.38 546.01
 80     80     80     80     80     80
  8.20
  3.47   4.36
 45.65  22.58 611.63
  6.39   3.16  44.62   7.32
  3.22   3.77  23.47   3.33   4.02
 45.58  22.01 548.00  40.99  21.43 585.14
 80     80     80     80     80     80
  5.74
  1.35   2.49
 39.24  12.73 535.30
```

```
  4.94    1.65  37.36    5.39
  1.67    2.32  15.71    1.85    3.06
 40.11   12.94 496.86   38.09   14.91 538.76
 80      80     80      80      80     80
END DATA
LISREL
 /"EX 9.3: GRADE 6 - SON'S AND PARENTS' REPORTS OF PARENTAL"
 /"              SOCIOECONOMIC CHARACTERISTICS"
   /DA NI=6
   /MO NX=6 NK=3 TD=SY
   /LK /TRFED TRMED TRFOC
   /FR LX 1 1 LX 2 2 LX 3 3 TD 2 1
   /VA 1 LX 4 1 LX 5 2 LX 6 3
   /OU SE TV MI ND=2
 /"EX 9.3: GRADE 9 - SON'S AND PARENTS' REPORTS OF PARENTAL"
 /"              SOCIOECONOMIC CHARACTERISTICS"
   /DA
   /MO LX=PS PH=IN TD=SY
   /LK /TRFED TRMED TRFOC
   /FR TD 2 1
   /EQ TD 1 4 4 TD 4 4
   /EQ TD 1 5 5 TD 5 5
   /EQ TD 1 6 6 TD 6 6
   /OU
 /"EX 9.3: GRADE 12 - SON'S AND PARENTS' REPORTS OF PARENTAL"
 /"              SOCIOECONOMIC CHARACTERISTICS"
   /DA
   /MO LX=PS PH=IN TD=SY
   /LK /TRFED TRMED TRFOC
   /EQ TD 1 4 4 TD 4 4
   /EQ TD 1 5 5 TD 5 5
   /EQ TD 1 6 6 TD 6 6
   /OU
FINISH
```

Besides the annotated LISREL example in the part of the manual that is called "Examples," there are other LISREL examples given in part A, under "PRELIS and LISREL within SPSS."

Index

Index